W9-CHJ-689

DIVINE APPOINTMENT WITH DESTINY!

**Step Into Your
End Time Destiny!**

DR. MORRIS CERULLO

This book or parts thereof may not be reproduced in any form without
written permission of Morris Cerullo World Evangelism.
All scripture references are from the King James version
of the Bible unless otherwise noted.
Copyright © 2001

Scripture references marked AMP are from the
Amplified Bible version.
Copyright © 1965 by Zondervan Publishing House.

Scripture references marked NIV are from the
New International version of the Bible.
Copyright © 1973, 1978, 1984 by the International Bible Society.

Scripture references marked NAS are from the New American Standard
version of the Bible. Copyright © 1960, 1962, 1963, 1968, 1971, 1972,
1973, 1975, 1977 by the Lockman Foundation.

Scripture references marked TLB are from the Living Bible.
Copyright © 1971, by Tyndale House Publishers, Wheaton, Illinois 60187.

All rights reserved.
Publised by

MORRIS CERULLO WORLD EVANGELISM
P.O. Box 85277 • San Diego, CA 92186
(858) 277-2200
E-mail: morriscerullo@mcwe.com
Website: www.mcwe.com
For 24 hours, 7 days a week Prayer: **1(858)HELPLINE**
4 3 5 - 7 5 4 6
HELPLINE FAX: 1-858-427-0555

INTERNATIONAL: 001-858 HELPLINE

MORRIS CERULLO WORLD EVANGELISM OF CANADA
P.O. Box 3600 • Concord, Ontario L4K-1B6
(905) 669-1788

MORRIS CERULLO WORLD EVANGELISM OF GREAT BRITAIN
P.O. Box 277 • Hemel Hempstead, HERTS HP2-7DH
44 (0)1 442 232432

Dedication

To all those who are hungry and ready to experience a full manifestation of all that God has ordained for His Church in this end-time hour.

Copyright © 1997
Printed 1997
Re-printed 2005
MORRIS CERULLO WORLD EVANGELISM
Printed in the United States of America

TABLE OF
CONTENTS

Introduction

I have carried this message God gave me for the Church for almost a year. It has been like liquid fire shut up within me.

Never before have I sensed such an urgency to release a message, and for the Church to rise up and take the position of power and authority God has planned it to have in this end-time hour.

Something must happen to the Church!

We are at a point of spiritual destiny when all that God has planned to be accomplished in and through His people will be fulfilled.

From the beginning of time, God had a destiny for His Church. For thousands of years this plan remained a mystery ...cherished and hidden away in God's heart until the time that He determined to reveal it. Then, at the appointed time, He unveiled it to the Apostle Paul by direct revelation.

Throughout the ages God's destiny for the Church has unfolded. Now, in this end-time hour before Christ returns for His Church, God is again speaking to the Church revealing what He plans to accomplish.

To step into the end-time spiritual destiny God has for the Church, we must have a fresh revelation, by His Spirit, directly from the heart of God. Not only must we have a fresh revelation of what God intended for His Church, we must also have a fresh manifestation and outpouring of the Power of the Holy Spirit to shake us out of our complacency and bring us to a position where there is a full demonstration and manifestation of God's power flowing through us to the world!

During the first three centuries, the Church experienced its greatest growth, but something happened in the third century that blocked the flow of God's power. From the third century until today, in the twentieth century, we have not seen the same powerful demonstration of the true power of Pentecost with signs, wonders, and miracles being manifested.

It's time to get the mask off!

In this book we will take a long, hard look at some of the reasons why the Church today is not operating in the powerful dimension God intended. We are going to look at the hindrances to the flow of God's power, and God's original intention and purpose for His Church.

If what we see in the Church today is all that God will do or all that He has planned to do in the Church, there is no hope for this world!

The time has come for the Church to face every weakness, every shortcoming, and every failure. We don't have time to keep sweeping things under the carpet.

God has an end-time prophetic destiny for the Church today.

You have a divine appointment with destiny!

My question to you is, "Are you ready to step into your end-time destiny?"

Now is God's time for the Church to get advanced knowledge through the Holy Spirit, to tap into the very mind of God, and to experience a supernatural manifestation taking us into the fullness of all that He planned for us in this end-time hour.

It is my prayer that as you read this book, the "eyes of your understanding" will be opened. I pray that you will be sensitive to hear what the Spirit of God is saying to the end-time Church. By His Spirit, God is calling you to look beyond your failures, and beyond your limitations, and beyond your man-made goals to see the awesome spiritual destiny He has planned for you.

God has spoken a prophetic word over your life:

> *Ye have not chosen me, but I have chosen you, and*
> *ordained you, that ye should go and bring forth fruit,*
> *and that your fruit should remain: that whatsoever ye*

shall ask of the Father in my name, he may give it you.

John 15:16

I challenge you, in Jesus' Name, to open your spirit wide and receive a fresh revelation of God's destiny for the Church and for you. Then, rise up and take your position...step into your end time spiritual destiny!

God's Servant,

Brother Cerullo

This is your Hour! See yourself today Not as man sees you, but as God sees you. Then, STEP Out Boldly to fulfill ALL God has Purposed for your Life. Ephesians 1:17-19

CHAPTER ONE

God Has A Destiny For You!

The Church stands on the brink of its great end-time spiritual destiny!

God's plan for His Church, conceived and formed within His own bosom before the foundation of the world, is now being fulfilled.

This is the Church's finest hour when we will see the culmination and manifestation of all God's purposes and promises concerning the Church.

This is the day the prophets prophesied about and longed to see!

We are living in the most exciting time in the history of the Church! With all my heart I can truthfully say I would rather be living today than any other time!

Jesus is coming!

I do not expect to die. I believe we are the end-time generation who will usher in the King of Kings and Lord of Lords! Unless it is God's will to take me home, I expect to be alive when the trumpet of God sounds, the clouds roll back and we see Christ coming in the clouds in all His power and glory.

God's Destiny For You...INVINCIBILITY!

God is a God of purpose, plan, design, and objectivity. Before the foundation of the earth, He planned to have a unique people, consecrated unto Himself, who would manifest His power and glory to the world.

He planned to give birth to a Church that would be a part of Himself, vitally united with Him, an extension of Himself...possessing His power and glory...**invincible**!

God set forth a spiritual destiny..."a predetermined course of events"...for the Church.

When God chose a people...Israel, he revealed Himself in His power and glory and established an everlasting covenant relationship with them. In the Old Testament, His relationship with Israel reveals and unfolds His plan and purpose for His Church.

God kept His plan for the Church hidden. It remained a mystery throughout the ages. Then, at the appointed time, He unveiled His plan. The Apostle Paul wrote concerning this mystery:

> *Making known to us the mystery (secret) of His will (of His plan, of His purpose). [And it is this:] In accordance with His good pleasure (His merciful intention) which He had previously purposed and set forth in Him (He planned) for the maturity of the times and the climax of the ages to unify all things and head them up and consummate them in Christ, (both) things in heaven and things on earth.*

Ephesians 1:9-10, AMP

We are living in this time to which Paul referred as the "climax of the ages" when God is bringing the Church to full maturity.

This is the time God will bring all things in heaven and in earth together..."head them up and consummate them in Christ." All things will be set in order and brought together in harmony with Him!

It is very important for you to remember that God planned the hour in which you and I live. He has an end-time plan and destiny for His Church, and you are a vital part of that plan.

God planned for His Church to be the single, most powerful force on earth, and that it operate in nothing less than a full manifestation of the power and fullness that is in Christ.

In His letter to the believers and disciples in Ephesus, Paul sums up God's plan of power and victory for His Church.

Paul said:

His intention was the perfecting and the full equipping of the saints (His consecrated people), [that they should do] the work of ministering toward building up Christ's body (the church). [That it might develop] until we all attain oneness in the faith and in the [full and accurate] knowledge of the Son of God; that [we might arrive] at really mature manhood (the completeness of personality which is nothing less than the standard height of Christ's own perfection) the measure of the stature of the fullness of the Christ and the completeness found in Him.

Ephesians 4:12-13, AMP

Do you see any provision in these Scriptures for failure or weakness? God plans for every member of the Body of Christ to be "perfected" and "fully equipped"!

He plans for the Church to grow up until we reach the full stature of Jesus Christ!

It's Harvest Time!

We are living in a time of harvest. Harvest is a time of ripening and growing to full maturity. It is a time of the greatest manifestation, when the seeds have grown and reproduced a crop that is fully ripened and ready to be reaped.

It's harvest time for the Church. We are living in the closing hours of time when God is bringing His Church to a place of full maturity where we are operating in a full manifestation of the power and authority of Christ! This maturity God planned is coming quickly, and will usher in the greatest harvest of souls the world has ever seen.

The true Church of Jesus Christ will rise in new strength...in the power and anointing of the Holy Spirit...to become the living, breathing, powerful, organism God intended for it to be!

God's Destiny For You – Divine Capability!

Two thousand years ago the Church was born in a mighty manifestation of God's power. God breathed His very life into 120 men and women who had gathered together in Jerusalem. In obedience to Jesus' final charge to*"...tarry ye in the city of Jerusalem, until ye be endued with power from on high"*(Luke 24:49), they were, *"...all with one accord in one place"*(Acts 2:1).

The Holy Spirit swept into that upper room like a rushing, mighty wind. It encircled and enveloped them.

The atmosphere was literally charged with the power and Presence of Almighty God.

Flames of fire appeared over their heads as an outward sign of the inward transformation that was taking place within them.

The Church - the body of believers gathered together - were infused with power. They received all that was necessary to function as Christ's Body upon the earth. They were given "dunamis" power...the same power and the same anointing Jesus received at the Jordan River before He began His ministry.

The Church received a unique characteristic giving it divine capability to produce the proof of the resurrection of Jesus Christ, the Son of the living God!

Jesus had told them:

> *But ye shall receive power, after that the Holy Ghost is come upon you: and ye shall be witnesses unto me throughout Jerusalem, and in all Judea, and in Samaria, and unto the uttermost part of the earth.*
>
> Acts 1:8

He had commissioned them:

Go ye therefore, and teach all nations, baptizing them in the name of the Father, and of the Son and of the Holy Ghost.
Matthew 28:19

They received a divine capability to fulfill the work Christ commissioned them to do!

The disciples and body of believers boldly proclaimed the Word, healed the sick, cast out demons and raised the dead. They turned the world upside down for God!

By the third century they had reached the entire known world with the Gospel of Jesus Christ!

Something happened after the third century and the Church lost that experience of Apostolic power. Today, we cannot find a true demonstration of that same manifestation...the fire of Pentecost.

It's missing!

What Happened To The Church?

The time has come for the Church to "take the mask off!"

We must be willing to take a long, honest, hard look at the true spiritual condition of the Church today. It's time to stop sweeping our weaknesses, mistakes, and failures "under the carpet." We must not be afraid to face these weaknesses and failures, try to cover them up, nor make excuses.

We cannot and must not face them in our natural strength. We must yield ourselves fully to the Holy Spirit and allow Him to remove the spiritual cataracts from our eyes, reveal these weak areas within the Church, and release a divine flow of His power into our lives.

We are going to take an honest look at some of the things which have happened in the Church that have taken us off the course God set for us. And, with God's direction and anointing we are going to face them and step forward into our end-time destiny.

Are you ready?

Are you hungry for God to take you into the fullness of all that He has planned for you?

In all my years of ministry, I have never been so fearful...so burdened...for the Church of Jesus Christ as I am today.

When we take the mask off and compare the Church of God's original plan and purpose, with what His Church actually is and represents today, we are so far off course that it will take a supernatural move of the Holy Spirit to bring us to the place where God intends for us to be.

Even with the revelation, all the great teaching and preaching that has come forth since the Church was born two thousand years ago, we are still spiritual "babies" in our comprehension concerning the Church.

A great percentage of Church members are living historical, psychosomatic Christianity. The personal spiritual breakthrough which brings them out of the natural realm into a living, vibrant relationship with Jesus where the life flow of God is released through them to the world...is missing!

The Church must have a fresh revelation of Jesus and see Him as He is today — seated at the right hand of the Father in a position of supreme power and authority. We must also have a full revelation of the true Church, where we understand what Christ has intended for it to be. This is the major purpose God directed me to write this book.

Until we have this revelation...not historical, not doctrinal, not what someone else has said...and God gives us a spiritual breakthrough where we grow up in our understanding and comprehension of Jesus Christ, and understand fully who we are and what God intended for His Church, we will never be able to fulfill the end-time spiritual destiny God has for us.

My Cry Is, "Oh God, Anoint Our Eyes!"

The Apostle Paul prayed continually for believers that God would give them a spirit of wisdom and revelation in the knowledge of Christ so they would know Him intimately.

> *(For I always pray) the God of our Lord Jesus Christ, the Father of Glory, that He may grant you a spirit of wisdom and revelation (of insight into mysteries and secrets) in the (deep and intimate) knowledge of Him, By having the eyes of your heart flooded with light, so that you can know and understand the hope to which He has called you and how rich is His glorious inheritance in the saints (His set apart ones).*

Ephesians 1:17-18, AMP

This is my prayer for you. I pray that as you read this book that a spirit of revelation and wisdom will flood your heart and mind. I pray that God will take you beyond the limitations of your natural mind and give you a full revelation of Himself and what He wants to do for you.

My prayer for you is that God will anoint your eyes, so that you will be able to see beyond the limitations that have been built in your mind...beyond the limited experience of the Church today...beyond your limited experience to see the spiritual destiny of His Church to which God has called you.

I pray that you will see, as never before, God has a spiritual destiny planned for you.

A New Level Of Spiritual Understanding

For hundreds of years the Church has been living far below the position of power and authority God planned for it. Through our lack of revelation knowledge we have allowed Satan to rob us of our spiritual inheritance.

But now in this time of spiritual destiny, God will bring us to a new level of spiritual maturity in our understanding. Not only will we have a full revelation of our rights and privileges as sons of God and joint heirs of the kingdom of God, we will rise to a new level of spiritual maturity in which we are taking our position as full grown sons and daughters who have grown to the full stature of Jesus Christ where Christ, in all His fullness, is manifested in us.

Already, in the Spirit, I can see this happening!

The true Church of Jesus Christ is rising to its feet!

For years, I have been prophesying that the Church will be raptured in an even greater position of power than it was born in.

Get ready!

This is your opportunity to become involved in the greatest hour in the history of the Church. This is not a time to sit back on the sidelines. It's time for you to become a participator...to move into action.

Don't make excuses that you are waiting until you feel you have reached a certain spiritual plateau where you feel you are spiritual or holy enough, or that you are waiting for God's power to somehow fall out of heaven upon you before you step out by faith.

It is time for you to hear the voice of God's Spirit calling you. It is time to make a new determination, that regardless of what it takes, you will not give up until you step into the end-time spiritual destiny God has for you!

Your Spiritual Destiny Is Based Upon The Infallible, Impregnable Word Of God!

"Spiritual destiny" is not just a catchy phrase or man-made slogan. It is not some ethereal, mystical concept. The word, "destiny" means "a predetermined course of events." The spiritual destiny God has for you is not a matter of happenstance or conjecture. It is real...something that you can grasp hold of and see manifested in your life.

The spiritual destiny God has planned for you is based upon the one thing in this world which cannot ever be shaken...the infallible, impregnable Word of the living God!

There never was a time in the history of the Church when the Word of God was more important!

We live in an age of mass communication and we have many voices speaking to us. One of the most popular things on television in the United States are the psychic hotlines. People are calling palm readers and psychics wanting to know what their future is. "When will I get my next girlfriend?" "When will I get my next raise?" "When will I find my future happiness?"

There are confusing spirits and spirits of the natural mind speaking to us from everywhere. Unless you know that the Word of God defies all human reasoning and goes beyond the natural man, you will be tossed to and fro.

When human reasoning takes the place of the naked reality of God's Word, you're in trouble!

To believe this takes naked faith...an incredible confirmation in your spirit that God is Who He said He is, that God said what He meant and meant what He said.

God needs people with simple, naked faith who will dare to believe, "If God said it, that's good enough for me!"

Regardless of who you are, God has a specific plan and purpose for your life. There are specific things and events He planned to take place in your life and He has specific purposes He wants to accomplish through you.

God has declared in His Word what He has planned to accomplish in your life, and He will bring it to pass!

God has said,

> ...I am God, and there is no other; I am God and there is none like me. I make known the end from the beginning, from ancient times, what is still to come. I

say: My purpose will stand, and I will do all that I please... What I have said, that will I bring about; what I have planned, that will I do.

Isaiah 46:9-11, NIV

God spoke through Isaiah,

So shall my word be that goeth forth out of my mouth: it shall not return unto me void, but it shall accomplish that which I please, and it shall prosper in the thing whereto I sent it.

Isaiah 55:11

You do not ever need to question or doubt. God will fulfill all that He has planned and purposed for His Church and for your life. Though everything else may fail, not one Word He has ever spoken will ever fail!

God is not a man, that he should lie; neither the son of man, that he should repent: hath he said, and shall he not do it? or hath he spoken and shall he not make it good?

Numbers 23:19

Not one Word that God has ever decreed over your life will ever return unto Him void. But, you must receive His Word into your Spirit and act upon it in faith before it will be accomplished and become a reality in your life.

- He has destined you to overcome Satan, sin, hell and the grave, and live in 100 percent victory, 100 percent of the time over 100 percent of the enemy's power! (1 John 4:4; 5:4-5)

- He has destined you to be conformed into the image of Christ! (Romans 8:29)

- He has destined you to grow up into the
  full stature of Jesus Christ!   (Ephesians 4:13)
- He has destined you to have His miracle
  power flowing through your life! (Acts 1:8)

- He has destined you to do the same works Jesus
  did, healing the sick, casting out devils, and
  loosing those who are bound by Satan!
  (John 14:12)

Your end-time future course of destiny has been set...

- He has destined you to be resurrected from the
  dead and rise to meet Him at His coming!
  (1 Thessalonians 4:16)

- He has destined you to rule and reign with Him
  for a thousand years! (Revelation 20:6)

- He has destined you to live with Him for eternity!
  (1 Thessalonians 4:17)

There are many Christians who live their entire lives and never fulfill the spiritual destiny God has planned for them.
They miss it!
There are many reasons why.
They may not know what God's purpose is for their lives, and how to respond and act in faith upon God's direction to make it happen.
There are many Christians today who are fearful, who are hesitating and holding back. They allow other things and people to distract and hinder them. Instead of acting on the direction and the Word they receive from God, they are

complacent and careless. They make excuses for their inactivity and lethargy.

God knows you intimately...everything about you. He knows the thoughts, intents, and desires of your heart. He knows your strengths, your weaknesses, and your failures. But He still has a purpose for you to fulfill.

You Have A Spiritual Destiny!

The prophet Jeremiah had a spiritual destiny.

Before He was born, God had a specific purpose for Him to fulfill. God spoke to Jeremiah,

...Before I formed thee in the belly I knew thee, and before thou camest forth out of the womb I sanctified thee, and I ordained thee a prophet unto the nations.

Jeremiah 1:5

God told Jeremiah that He knew him before he was conceived. He knew who Jeremiah was going to be because He had a purpose for him to fulfill. He sanctified, set him apart, and ordained him as a prophet sent to the nations.

God had a claim on Jeremiah's life prior to any other earthly relationships. Jeremiah was chosen and set apart for a specific spiritual purpose God had determined. He had a spiritual destiny!

The Apostle Paul had a spiritual destiny!

He was the chief persecutor of the believers in the Early Church. He had been given the authority from the chief priests to bind all those who were followers of Christ.

Paul had been creating havoc in the Church, entering into houses, gathering up men and women, binding them and putting them in prison. (Acts 8:3)

But God had a spiritual destiny for Paul. He knew him and saw his persecution of the Church. On the road to

Damascus, Paul had a supernatural encounter with Christ. He had a personal revelation of Christ. He responded to the call of God and set his mind to fulfill the divine purpose of God. He made a 180 degree turn from chief persecutor of the Church to become one of the chief apostles of the Lord.

A young Jewish woman named Esther had a spiritual destiny!

God had a purpose for her life. He positioned her to be an instrument in saving the nation of Israel from destruction.

As we look more closely at the lives of these three individuals, we will discover major keys and specific steps that enabled them to fulfill their spiritual destiny, and how you can apply these keys in your life.

You may not be called to be a prophet, pastor, teacher or to fill some major leadership role within the Church. However, regardless of who you are, if you have been born again by the Spirit of the living God, you have a spiritual destiny.

You may be unsettled in your mind, uncertain as to what God's purpose is for your life.

You may have a calling upon your life and you have not moved into the spiritual destiny God has for you. You are waiting for a more opportune time or for everything to somehow fall into place before you act on His direction to you.

God is not depending upon your limited natural abilities. He wants to empower you and use you to minister to the needs of those around you, and to fulfill His plan and purposes in this end-time hour.

Are You Ready To Step Into Your End-time Destiny?

The spiritual destiny God has planned for you will not happen simply because you want it!

It will not happen unless you dare to believe God will do all He has promised.

It will not happen unless you act upon His promises.

You must be willing to STEP INTO IT!

You must recognize it, accept it and take steps of faith in obedience to whatever God directs you to do.

It will not be easy.

It will cost you something.

It will take a new, stronger dedication and commitment greater than you have ever made.

You must be willing to lay aside any preconceived ideas and man-made strategies and walk in new, uncharted territory.

As you walk in obedience to what God directs you to do, there will be times when you will be misunderstood or criticized. However, you must be willing to face all opposition and continue on the course God has set before you without wavering.

Once you really see with your spiritual eyes what God has planned for you, you cannot remain the same!

You will begin to live your life with a new sense of purpose and excitement. You will keep this vision before you...set it before you as a goal.

On the job...when you walk down the street... sitting in your home with your family...you will be aware of who you are as a child of God and what God will accomplish in your life as you yield to His Spirit working within you!

This is the time for you to settle in your heart and mind and make a full commitment that you will step into the end-time spiritual destiny God has for you.

Keep your spiritual focus and don't allow anyone or anything to hinder or stop you from stepping into your end-time spiritual destiny!

It is time for the Church to come face to face with its end-time destiny. We are going to take the mask off and look at where the Church has failed to step into its spiritual destiny and what God is revealing to us that He wants to accomplish within us in this end-time harvest.

What is God's end-time destiny for His Church?

What has God planned for you as a vital part of His end-time destiny?

CHAPTER TWO

Beyond Natural Limitations

During the course of my over fifty-six years of ministry, God has spoken to me many times with a prophetic message, exhortation or warning for the Body of Christ.

A few short months before entering the decade of the 90s, God spoke to me and gave me one of the most awesome, unique, challenging prophecies He has ever given me for the Body of Christ.

God's Word is clear that He does not do anything without revealing it to His prophets. *"Surely the Lord God will do nothing, but he revealeth his secret unto his servants the prophets"* (Amos 3:7). God reveals events and things which are going to happen to prepare us. When He speaks a prophetic word through His servants, the prophets, before it happens and then it comes to pass, He receives the glory.

In September of 1989, I made my first trip to minister to the Australian people. Theresa and I had just left Perth and were in Sydney, where we were staying overnight. We were tired from the crusade and had arrived at our room in Sydney at about 4:00 or 5:00 o'clock in the afternoon. We decided we would just take a little rest before we went out for dinner. We got into bed.

God spoke to me, "Morris, get up!" I got up from my bed and went into the next room. God spoke again, "Write." Then He began to pour out revelation after revelation regarding five major crises and five tremendous waves of the Holy Spirit which were coming in the decade of the nineties.

It was during that time God spoke to me and revealed that the 90s was His Decade of Destiny and the Decade of the Holy Spirit.

When God revealed that the 90's was His decade of the Holy Spirit, I wrestled with it for a long time. But, then the Lord showed that He was not talking theologically, but prophetically, saying, "This is My

Decade of the Holy Spirit." He showed me that during this decade the Holy Spirit will accomplish major purposes within the Body of Christ.

One of the major changes God showed me would take place within the structure of the organized church. God will break man's traditional barriers that are hindering the Church from operating as He intended. Many Christians, including pastors and Christian leaders, will find it very difficult to accept and cope with these changes.

Then, in the middle of 1995, in the month of August, God spoke to me and said, "Son, this decade of the Holy Spirit is about to close."

I asked God, "How can a decade close in the middle?" God said,

"Since the birth of My Church, when true Pentecostal power was manifested, My Church has not manifested this power. But the time has come, in My end time harvest time where I will again restore and release this wave of Pentecostal power."

A new wave of Pentecostal power will sweep over those who want to be part of God's end time plan. God has been waiting to literally pour this out.

God said, "Before this decade closes, there will be a tremendous manifestation of my true Holy Spirit power and it will last for three years."

Get yourself positioned!

God is about to unveil a greater power and glory than the Church has ever known. What is coming is awesome!

God is saying, "I'm going to do a new work among My people! There will be a new release...a new demonstration of my supernatural power."

A divine capability will once again be given to God's people...to show the world that Jesus Christ is the all-powerful Son of the living God, and that there is salvation, healing and deliverance in His Name!

A Continual Flow Of God's Unlimited Power!

God never intended the power and anointing of the Holy Spirit that was released at Pentecost to diminish. He never intended His miracle-working power, or the gifts of the Spirit to cease functioning within the Church.

God intends there to be a continual flow of His unlimited, immeasurable power within His people today!

God raised up the Church for a divine purpose. Just as He raised up the Jews and manifested His supernatural power in their lives through signs, wonders and miracles as a witness to show the world that Jehovah is the great, "I AM," He raised up the Church, placed His supernatural miracle-working power within it as a witness to the world that Jesus is Who he claims to be, the Son of the living God!

What has happened to the Church?

Men have placed narrow limitations upon God and the working of the Spirit. We have tried to confine the unlimited, immeasurable power of Almighty God within a structure based upon our natural, limited understanding, man-made traditions and ideologies.

God has an end time destiny for you! He never intended to place any limitations upon the release of His power through you!

You are destined to be a man or woman of power and authority, through whom His unlimited power flows unhindered in a full manifestation. As this awesome manifestation of God's true Pentecostal power is released, there will be a flow...a gushing forth of His Spirit within you to heal the sick, cast out devils, raise the dead and fulfill His will in this end time hour.

Jesus said that out of our innermost beings will flow rivers of living water!

He who believes in Me — who cleaves to and trusts in and relies on me — as the Scripture has said, Out from his being springs and rivers of living water shall flow (continuously).

John 7:38, AMP

31

Jesus wasn't talking about an occasional release of His power and anointing that would come upon you, and then leave. He was talking about a continual flow of the unlimited power that remains in you through the Holy Spirit!

When you are baptized with the Holy Spirit, there will be a life-giving river of God's power continually being released through you. The power of God will flow out of you as the natural result of the indwelling of the Holy Spirit. Wherever you go, His power will flow out of you to bring healing and deliverance. As long as you remain yielded to the Holy Spirit, that unlimited power of God will flow freely through you.

Are you ready to step into your end time destiny?

Are you ready for a revolution in your spiritual life?

Look Beyond Your Natural Limitations

Before you can step into that destiny, you must look beyond your natural limitations.

Every individual who has ever been used by God was required to act upon what God directed them to do. If they failed to act on God's direction, they failed to lay claim to the destiny God planned for them.

The Prophet Jeremiah, the Apostle Paul and Queen Esther stepped into their destinies. At strategic moments in their lives, they responded in faith and acted upon the direction God gave them. They acted upon the Word of the Lord spoken to them.

You will not be able to see the spiritual destiny God has planned for your life fulfilled unless you take steps of faith. If you don't take those steps, you will miss your spiritual destiny!

As we look closely at the lives of Jeremiah, Paul and Esther, you will see the steps of faith they took in fulfilling the purposes of God in their lives.

Look at Jeremiah's response to the Word of the Lord he received, that God was ordaining and sending him forth as a prophet to the nations. He was the son of a priest, and estimated to be about twenty years of age when God called him.

Jeremiah told God, *"Ah, Lord God! Behold, I cannot speak, for I am only a youth"* (Jeremiah 1:6, AMP).

The first things Jeremiah faced were the natural limitations he placed upon himself. He had a limited concept of what he could do.

Have you ever made excuses to God concerning what He has called you to do because of your natural limitations?

When God called Moses to lead the children of Israel out of Egyptian bondage, Moses hesitated and made excuses because of his own natural limitations. He said, "Oh Lord, I have never been eloquent, neither in the past nor since you have spoken to your servant. I am slow of speech and tongue."

God told him, "Who gave man his mouth? Who makes him deaf or mute? Who gives him sight or makes him blind? Is it not I, the Lord? Now go; I will help you speak and teach you what to say."

Even though God promised Moses that He would supernaturally enable him and would give him the words to speak, Moses still hesitated. He told God, *"O Lord, please send someone else to do it"* (Exodus 4:10-14, NIV).

The Lord was angry with Moses and appointed Moses' brother, Aaron, to be his spokesman. Moses was greatly used by God, but in this one area failed to achieve all that God had planned for him because his eyes were on his own limitations.

You have a spiritual destiny God wants to fulfill in your life. Whatever God directs you to do, do not be bound nor hesitate to obey Him because of your own weaknesses, inabilities or handicaps.

God is not looking at who you are, with all your limitations. He is looking at what He can make of you!

Stop using your weaknesses and inabilities as an excuse!

Step into your spiritual destiny by looking beyond your natural limitations, and by believing God to supernaturally enable you to do all that He has asked you to do and fulfill His purposes in your life.

God called Jeremiah to be a prophet to the nations, but he had a very limited understanding of what God could do through him. He saw himself as a young man...unable to speak. The enormity of the task before him...of being a prophet...speaking as God's spokesman to the nations, was beyond what he perceived himself capable of doing.

How do you see yourself?

Do you only see yourself with your limited natural abilities, or do you see yourself as God intended you to be through the power of the Holy Spirit working in your life?

Always remember, whenever God chooses and calls anyone, He does not ever make a mistake! Whoever you are and whatever He calls you to do, He will empower and equip you with the divine enablement to accomplish his purposes.

Cast Out Every Trace Of Fear!

When Jeremiah heard what God wanted him to do as part of his spiritual destiny, he faced another major obstacle...FEAR!

God met Jeremiah's hesitation and fear with reassurance and a promise. He said, *"Do not say, 'I am only a child.' You must go to everyone I send you to and say whatever I command you. Do not be afraid of them, for I am with you and will rescue you"* (Jeremiah 1:7-8, NIV).

As a prophet of God, speaking the Word of the Lord, Jeremiah would face great opposition and would be severely persecuted, but God told him not to fear. Fear is one of Satan's tools to keep you from fulfilling the calling of God upon your life!

- Fear will paralyze your faith!
- Fear will cause you to disobey God!
- Fear will stop you from doing the works of God!

To step into the spiritual destiny God has for you, you must cast out every trace of fear!

- Fear of man must go!
- Fear of what others will say or do, must go!
- Fear of failure must go!
- Fear of your own natural limitations must go!

The fear of man is a trap.

> *The fear of man bringeth a snare: but whoso putteth his trust in the Lord shall be safe.*
>
> Proverbs 29:25

Once you allow fear to take hold in your life, instead of living your life to please God, you will be living to please man.

In these final moments before Christ's return, God is going to use those who are fearless...bold...daring!

He will use those who are listening to hear His direction, and once they hear Him speaking, they will boldly step out in faith and trust God to fulfill His word.

The key to the fearlessness God wants you to have is knowing God's Presence is with you to make you victorious. God told Jeremiah, *"Do not be afraid of them, for I am with you and will rescue you"* (Jeremiah 1:8, NIV).

When you know God has spoken to you...
Know that He has called and sent you...
Know that He has anointed you...
Know that He has empowered you...
Know that He is with you to fight for you and give you victory in every circumstance...
You will not be fearful!

Walk In God's Authority!

With the commission God gave Jeremiah, He gave him His authority. Jeremiah said,

> *Then the LORD reached out his hand and touched my mouth and said to me, "Now, I have put my words in your mouth. See, today I appoint you over nations and kingdoms to uproot and tear down, to destroy and overthrow, to build and to plant.*
>
> Jeremiah 1:9-10, NIV

God touched Jeremiah's mouth as a tangible expression that He had empowered him. From that day forward, the words God directed Jeremiah to speak were accompanied with God's power and authority to accomplish all that he spoke.

God's words in his mouth were all the authority he needed to do the work God had called him to do as a prophet:

- To root out!
- To pull down!
- To destroy and throw down!
- To build!
- To plant!

With the calling and commission from God comes His anointing...His power and authority to fulfill His purposes. There is no reason why you should ever be fearful as long as you know He has given you His power and authority to accomplish whatever He has called you to do.

To step into your spiritual destiny you must forget your natural limitations, stop leaning to the arm of the flesh and fulfill all that God calls you to do in His power and authority!

Jesus promised, *"Behold, I give you power to tread on serpents and scorpions, and over all the power of the enemy..."* (Luke 10:19).

He said, *"Whatsoever ye shall bind on earth shall be bound in heaven: and whatsoever ye shall loose on earth shall be loosed in heaven"* (Matthew 18:18).

He promised, *"And these signs shall follow them that believe; In my name shall they cast out devils; they shall speak with new tongues...they shall lay hands on the sick and they shall recover"* (Mark 16:17, 18).

He has promised you, *"But ye shall receive power, after that the Holy Ghost is come upon you: and ye shall be witnesses unto me..."* (Acts 1:8).

These verses will be like fire "shut up in your bones" by the time you finish this book.

The time has come when the Church of Jesus Christ must boldly go forward, in the power and authority Christ has intended, to bring in a great end time harvest of souls before He comes.

One of the reasons why we do not see more demons being cast out, more people being delivered and set free from drugs, alcohol, sexual perversion; more of God's miracle power being released with blind eyes being opened and the lame walking, is because the Church has not been operating in the power and authority God intended!

The majority of Christians, including pastors and Christian leaders have been trying to fulfill God's calling upon their lives, in their own strength, instead of through the power and authority of the Holy Spirit flowing through them.

In this end time hour, there must come a new release of God's divine power and authority flowing through us to meet the needs of the lost and dying in our churches, homes, cities, and nations!

Four Major Steps You Must Take

There are four things God instructed Jeremiah to do to step into his spiritual destiny: God said:

> *Get yourself ready! Stand up and say to them whatever I command you. Do not be terrified by them, or I will terrify you before them."*
>
> Jeremiah 1:17, NIV

1. The call of God is always a call to aggressive action.

To fulfill the ministry God called him to, required nothing less than total commitment to God. God told Jeremiah, "Get yourself ready!" He was being sent as a prophet to proclaim and warn of God's judgments upon Judah. His message was not one that the people wanted to hear, and he was going to face the persecution and opposition of the kings, officials, priests and people.

Regardless of what God's calling is upon your life, to step into your spiritual destiny, you must spiritually prepare yourself for aggressive action! You must be prepared to face the resistance and opposition of the enemy!

You must be prepared to make a full commitment and dedication of yourself to fulfill the work God has given you to do. You must be ready to make whatever sacrifices necessary!

2. Rise up!

God's call to Jeremiah required an immediate response. He told him, "Stand up and say to them whatever I command you." There could be no passivity or reluctance in acting upon what God had directed him to do. It was necessary for Jeremiah to move into action...to accept and take his position as God's prophet and begin to speak the message God gave him to speak.

To step into your spiritual destiny, you must accept the position of ministry God has given you and move into action! You cannot remain in a state of passivity or indecision.

When God reveals what He wants you to do, you must put your faith into action. Rise up, without hesitation, and begin to do it in the power and authority He has given you. "Just do it!"

3. Speak what God commands you to speak!

This required a daring boldness and unwavering, unyielding faithfulness to God. Jeremiah was required to be obedient in speaking all that God directed him to speak, regardless of the opposition he faced. He had to be willing to face the people, kings and priests and speak words of rebuke, condemnation, warning, and judgment.

To step into your spiritual destiny, you must have this same daring boldness and faithfulness to God in fulfilling all He has called you to do. Regardless of the personal cost to you, you must be obedient.

You must speak what He directs you to speak, do what He says do, go where and when He says go.

4. Be not afraid!

God commanded Jeremiah not to be afraid of those he would face or He would allow him to become overcome by them. He said, "Do not be terrified of them or I will terrify you before them." God promised to be with Jeremiah. The key to his fearlessness and victory is found in verse nineteen. God promised him,

> *They will fight against you but will not overcome you, for I am with you and will rescue you,"* *declares the Lord.*
>
> Jeremiah 1:19, NIV

To step into your spiritual destiny and fulfill God's purposes, you cannot be fearful or you will be overcome by the enemy. Your victory is assured and you will overcome every obstacle as long as your faith is focused upon the fact that God's Presence is with you to make you victorious.

As you step into the end-time spiritual destiny God has for you, you must be prepared to face opposition.

There will be obstacles you will have to overcome.

There will be those who will not understand what God is directing you to do, or the message He has given you to speak.

There will be those who will reject you, reject your message, and try to block or place obstacles in your way to stop you from accomplishing the work God has called you to do.

Expect opposition, and be prepared to face it in the power of the Holy Spirit.

You must not allow intimidation, discouragement or opposition to stop you!

God Requires Total Obedience

For a moment let us now look at the Apostle Paul's life to see what steps he took in fulfilling the spiritual destiny God planned for him.

Paul, on his way to Damascus, was determined to find the followers of Christ, bind them and bring them bound to Jerusalem. But, God had a divine purpose for his life. Paul had a spiritual destiny!

On the road to Damascus, Christ revealed Himself to Paul and asked him, *"...Saul, Saul, why persecutest thou me?"* [Paul's immediate response was], *"...Lord, what wilt thou have me to do?"* (Acts 9:4&6).

There, on that road, Christ called Paul and revealed His divine purposes for his life. He told Paul:

> *But rise, and stand upon thy feet: for I have appeared unto thee for this purpose, to make thee a minister and a witness both of these things which thou hast seen, and of those things in the which I will appear unto thee; Delivering thee from the people, and from the Gentiles, unto whom I now send thee, To open their eyes, and to turn them from darkness to light, and from the power of Satan unto God, that they may receive forgiveness of sins, and inheritance among them which are sanctified by faith that is in me.*

> Acts 26:16-18

Notice Paul's immediate response to the Lord, "What do you want me to do?" At that moment in the awesome Presence of the Lord, Paul was willing...totally submitted to do whatever Christ wanted him to do.

Are you willing, totally submitted to whatever Christ reveals that He wants to accomplish in and through you?

Don't hesitate or waver. Make a new commitment and dedication to respond in faith to all that God directs. Be ready to act the moment He speaks.

Without hesitation, Paul stepped into his spiritual destiny. He obeyed the Lord's instructions to go into Damascus and wait for further instructions.

In that holy encounter on the road to Damascus, Christ clearly revealed to Paul His purpose for his life. Christ told him, *"...I have appeared unto thee for this purpose..."* (Acts 26:16).

He told Paul to rise up...to prepare for aggressive action because he was making him a minister; and from that day forward, was sending him as an apostle to the Gentiles.

    1. Christ was making him a minister and a witness of both the things he had seen, and those things which Christ was going to reveal to him.

2. He was sending Paul to the Gentiles to open their eyes and turn them from darkness to light.

3. He was commissioning Paul to turn them from the dominion and power of Satan unto God so they would receive forgiveness of sins.

Paul stepped into his spiritual destiny through his life of obedience in doing all that God directed him to do. When he later related his experience to King Aggripa he said, *"I was not disobedient unto the heavenly vision"* (Acts 26:19).

While Paul was in Damascus, the Lord spoke to Ananias in a vision and sent him to Paul. When he laid hands on him, Paul received his sight and was filled with the Holy Spirit!

Paul stepped into his spiritual destiny by going forward in the power and authority of the Holy Spirit. For several days he remained with the disciples in Damascus and immediately began to proclaim the Gospel of Jesus Christ.

> *And when he had received meat, he was strengthened. Then was Saul certain days with the disciples which were at Damascus. And straightway he preached Christ in the synagogues, that he is the Son of God. But all that heard him were amazed, and said; Is not this he that destroyed them which called on this name in Jerusalem, and came hither for that intent, that he might bring them bound unto the chief priests? But Saul increased the more in strength, and confounded the Jews which dwelt at Damascus, proving that this is very Christ.*
>
> Acts 9:19-22

What is the vision...the purpose...the spiritual destiny...God wants to fulfill in your life? Can you say, like the Apostle Paul, "I have not been disobedient to the purpose God has given me to fulfill?"

If you still do not know the purpose "the spiritual destiny" God has for your life, this is your time to find it and move into what God has for you. As you read this book, I

41

believe God will reveal His end-time destiny to you. Keep your spirit open wide and allow God to speak to you.

If you feel that you have made too many mistakes ...too many failures...and have missed your spiritual destiny, it's not too late!

Ask God's forgiveness, rise up...take aggressive action ...go in his power and authority!

Your Life Must Become A Seed!

Queen Esther stepped into her spiritual destiny through her willingness to lay down her life. A decree by King Ahasuerus had gone forth throughout the land to destroy all the Jews, including women and young children, in one day. There was great mourning and fasting among the Jews over this decree.

Mordecai instructed Esther to go before the king and make supplication on behalf of her people.

Esther had a spiritual destiny! Mordecai told her,

> *Who knows but that you have come to the kingdom for such a time as this and for this very occasion?*

> Esther 4:14,AMP

God raised Esther up to fulfill this purpose and use her as an instrument to save the nation of Israel from destruction.

There was a law that if anyone came before the king without being summoned, or without his permission, they would be put to death unless the king extended the golden scepter toward them. Esther rose up in the Spirit and took aggressive action! She called a three-day fast among all the Jews before presenting herself to the king.

She stepped into her spiritual destiny by putting her life on the line. She told Mordecai,

> *...So will I go in unto the king, which is notaccording to the law: and if I perish, I perish.*

> Esther 4:16

Esther committed herself one-hundred percent to the divine purpose God had called her to fulfill at that crucial moment when the Jewish people were ready to be destroyed.

To step into the spiritual destiny God has for your life, you must have this same strong dedication and commitment where you are willing to lay your life down in fulfilling His calling upon your life.

This is the most important prerequisite to seeing the fulfillment of all that God has planned to accomplish in your life.

Jesus said,

> ...*Except a corn of wheat fall into the ground and die, it abideth alone: but if it die, it bringeth forth much fruit. He that loveth his life shall lose it; and he that hateth his life in this world shall keep it unto life eternal.*
>
> John 12:24-25

Your life must become as a seed which is sown into good soil. Only as you are willing to die to your own will, your desires, your plans, your goals, will God's Spirit flow through you to produce spiritual fruit.

Only as you lose your life for Christ's sake and the Gospel, will His life be released within you to minister salvation, healing, and deliverance to a lost and dying world.

Are you willing for your life to be a seed that falls into the ground and dies? If you are, there are no limits to what God can and will do through you.

Get rid of every limitation you have placed upon yourself, every human limitation and every limitation you have placed on God.

Get rid of everything in your life which will block the flow of God's Spirit. Make yourself available as an instrument to be used by God.

God Requires Absolute Total Surrender

There is a price to pay in order to have the power of God operating in your life. The Old Testament and New

Testament prophets paid a price and you and I must also pay a price.

Now, please do not misunderstand what I am saying. We cannot buy the power of God, but we must pay the price before God's power will work in and through us.

What is that price?

You must be willing to crucify your fleshly desires and goals. You must nail them to the cross of Calvary. It is a complete dying of self that will make you ready for the Master's use.

Abraham stepped into his spiritual destiny. God planned for him to be the father of many nations. He promised Abraham,

> *...a father of many nations have I made thee. And I will make thee exceeding fruitful, and I will make nations of thee, and kings shall come out of thee.*

> Genesis 17:5-6

Abraham paid the price when, in obedience to God, he was willing to offer up his only son through whom God had promised to bless and multiply his seed. The sacrifice God required of Abraham was not his son's life, because He sent an angel to stop him from sacrificing Isaac.

The sacrifice God required was one of total surrender of everything on earth which was valuable to Abraham. In the New Testament we see the same requirement:

> *Then Jesus said to his disciples, If any one desires to be My disciple, let him deny himself [disregard, lose sight of, and forget himself and his own interests] and take up his cross and follow Me (cleave steadfastly to me, conform wholly to My example in living and, if need be, in dying, also).*
> Matthew 16:24, AMP

Jesus does not mean everyone to literally despise and forsake their houses and families, although some will be called to be missionaries and evangelists. Jesus does require us, however, to be willing to surrender all our dreams and plans for our future. Before God can fulfill what He has planned to do in our lives, every fleshly, carnal desire must be forsaken.

In this time of self-crucifixion, you will find something amazing taking place. You will die a weak, powerless individual and will arise in a new strength and power you never dreamed was possible.

It is only in this process of dying that God will bring forth the fruit He desires.

The reason why the power of God flowed hrough the Apostle Paul in such a great measure is that he had found this place in God where he could say,

> *I am crucified with Christ: nevertheless I live; yet not I, but Christ liveth in me: and the life which I now live in the flesh I live by the faith of the Son of God, who loved me, and gave himself for me.*
>
> Galatians 2:20

We, too, must be willing to come to this place in absolute, total surrender, where our lives are lost... consumed in God's will.

Dying isn't easy. It is painful.

However, when we are willing to say good-bye to self; good-bye to fleshly desires; good-bye to the world and its temptations; then and only then, will Christ's life be produced in us. This will not be accomplished by any striving within ourselves, but by the faith of the Almighty Son of God who lives in us.

The cry of our hearts must be, *["He must increase, But I must decrease"]* (John 3:30).

Knowing Christ's coming is near, you must rise up with a new daring, a boldness, a new commitment, and go forward in the power and authority of Christ to fulfill His purposes in these closing moments of time!

God has a spiritual destiny for you...whatever you do, don't miss it!

Find what God has purposed for your life and focus on that purpose. Whatever purpose God has given you, He will fulfill it, if you are willing! Once He has purposed something, there is absolutely nothing that can stop it. Isaiah said,

> *For the Lord of hosts hath purposed, and who shall disannul it? and his hand is stretched out, and who shall turn it back?*
>
> Isaiah 14:27

How far do you want to go?

Are you content to remain where you are, or are you hungry to know and experience a full manifestation...a full release...of all God has ordained for you in this end-time hour?

If you are hungry...

If you are ready for God to do whatever is necessary to bring you into the fulfillment of all He intends for you to be...

If you are ready to rid yourself of every human limitation...

If you want to know the end-time destiny God plans for His Church in this end-time harvest...

Read on!

CHAPTER THREE

Unveiling The Mystery Of The Church

The Church of Jesus Christ is perhaps the greatest mystery of the ages.

God's plan of redemption through Christ and the establishment of the Church was conceived and born in the very heart of God, in eternity, before the foundation of the world.

The establishment of the Church was not accidental. It was not created haphazardly or something which happened on the spur of the moment. God not only planned for the Church to be established, He set the specific time when He would give it birth, and when He will bring it to full maturity.

In his letters to the Ephesian Church, the Apostle Paul revealed this great mystery of God's end-time plan. He said,

> *Making known to us the mystery (secret) of His will (of His plan, of His purpos). (And it is this:) In accordance with His good pleasure (His merciful intention) which He had previously purposed and set forth in Him, (He planned) for the maturity of the times and the climax of the ages to unify all things and head them up and consummate them in Christ, (both) things in heaven and things on the earth.*

Ephesians 1:9-10, AMP

The word "mystery" Paul used in these verses is translated from the Greek word "musterion." This word, in the New Testament, denotes not the mysterious, but that which can only be made known by revelation, by the Holy Spirit. It refers to that which cannot be comprehended through the natural mind.

47

In eternity, even before the foundation of the earth, Almighty God had a desire and longing within His heart to have a people for Himself, who would be called by His Name. He desired sons and daughters who would bear His image...who would share His very life, His nature, His purpose, His vision and be fully conformed to His will.

From this great desire in the heart of God, a plan developed. God planned to have a people who would stand in the full stature of Jesus Christ... possessing His life, His anointing, His power and authority, His faith, His mind, His wisdom, His righteousness, and His love.

God planned for us to be changed and transformed into Christ's image where we will be a full manifestation of His life to the world.

This is your destiny and mine!

Paul said:

> *...Even as (in His love) He chose us [actually picked us out for Himself as His own] in Christ before the foundation of the world, that we should be holy (consecrated and set apart for Him) blameless in His sight, even above reproach, before Him in love. For He foreordained us (destined us, planned in love for us) to be adopted (revealed) as His own children through Jesus Christ, in accordance with the purpose of His will [because it pleased Him and was His kind intent]. In Him we also were made (God's) heritage (portion) and we obtained an inheritance; for we had been foreordained (chosen and appointed beforehand) in accordance with His purpose, Who works out everything in agreement with the counsel and design of His (own) will, so that we who first hoped in Christ [who first put our confidence in Him have been destined and appointed] to live for the praise of His glory!*
>
> Ephesians 1:4-5s, 11-12, AMP

In the eternal purpose of God, He determined that all who believe on His Son would not only be redeemed from sin, but that they would bear His likeness, have His Spirit living within them and be incorporated into one Body through Christ.

God destined and planned for us to be "adopted" as His very own children through Jesus Christ! Under Roman law, an adopted son enjoyed the same status and privileges as a real son. Christ is God's Son by nature. Believers are sons by adoption, and are made joint-heirs with Christ.

We are destined, through our union with Christ, to be sons and daughters of God possessing the full rights of Sonship as Joint Heirs with Christ! Paul said

> *...but for ye have received the Spirit of adoption, whereby we cry, Abba, Father. The Spirit itself beareth witness with our spirit, that we are the children of God: and if children, then heirs; heirs of God, and joint - heirs with Christ...*

Romans 8:15-17

It was from this ultimate intention and purpose for the Church, God created the world and placed man upon it to take authority and rule over it. The world was brought into existence with this ultimate purpose in mind.

The Mystery Of The Church Was Reserved In The Heart Of God

God's eternal purpose was kept hidden, cherished within His heart until the time He determined to reveal it. Not even the Angels and principalities in heaven knew His purpose and plan. God's servants, the prophets He raised up in Israel, did not fully know this divine mystery. It remained a mystery even though

49

God revealed it, in part, through prophecies He spoke through them.

From God's promise to Abraham in Genesis 12:3 to make him and his seed a great nation, throughout the ages until God's designated time, the prophets prophesied concerning Christ, His sufferings, redemption, the indwelling of His Spirit, and the blessings to come. They diligently searched trying to determine the time when these things would come to pass and to whom these blessings would come. But, the mystery was not fully revealed to them. By His Spirit, God revealed that these prophecies were not for the time in which they were living, but were for a people and time yet to come.

The Apostle Peter told the believers;

> *The prophets who prophesied of the grace (divine blessing)which was intended for you, searched and inquired earnestly about this salvation. They sought (to find out) to whom or when this was to come which the Spirit of Christ working within them indicated when He predicted the sufferings of Christ and the glories that should follow (them). It was then disclosed to them that the services they were rendering were not meant for themselves and their period of time, but for you. (It is these very) things which have now already been made known plainly to you by those who preached the good news (the Gospel) to you by the (same) Holy Spirit sent from heaven. Into these things (the very) angels long to look!*

1 Peter 1:10-12, AMP

The angels in heaven longed to know this great mystery. Peter said, *"Into these things (the very) angels long to look"* (1 Peter 1:12).

Daniel was given a glimpse of the Church when God revealed to him an indestructible kingdom Christ would establish, which the saints would possess that would never be destroyed. In a dream He saw Christ standing before the "Ancient of Days."

> *And there was given him dominion, and glory, and a kingdom, that all people, nations, and languages, should serve him: his dominion is an everlasting dominion, which shall not pass away, and his kingdom that which shall not be destroyed.*
>
> Daniel 7:14

> *And the kingdom and dominion, and the greatness of the kingdom under the whole heaven, shall be given to the people of the saints of the most High, whose kingdom is an everlasting kingdom, and all dominions shall serve and obey him.*
>
> Daniel 7:27

The prophets knew through the revelations they received by the Spirit, God would one day send Christ to redeem a people for Himself and that His Spirit would dwell within them. But, His great plan and purpose for the Church remained a mystery. They did not know that God planned to join both Jews and Gentiles into one body, by His Spirit, forming "one new man."

> *By abolishing in His (own crucified) flesh the enmity caused by the Law with its decrees and ordinances [which He annulled]; that He from the two might create in Himself one new man [one new quality of humanity out of the two] so making peace.*
>
> Ephesians 2:15, AMP

Then, God unveiled the mystery to the Apostle Paul through direct revelation of the Holy Spirit. This mystery was one which could not be understood with man's natural mind. Paul did not learn it from any natural source.

It remained a mystery, hidden away, reserved in the heart of God until the fullness of time when He made it known to Paul. Paul was the first to receive this great revelation. He was called and anointed by God to unveil it and make it plain, so everyone would have a full understanding of His ultimate purpose for the Church.

God Unveiled The Mystery

This mystery concerning the Church, which had been concealed throughout the ages, unknown even by the angelic hosts of heaven, God revealed to all through the Apostle Paul. What had been withheld from the angelic hosts, was openly declared to the Church!

Paul said:

> ...*the mystery (secret) was made known to me and I was allowed to comprehend it by direct revelation, as I already briefly wrote you, when you read this you can understand my insight into the mystery of Christ. (This mystery) was never disclosed to human beings in past generations as it has now been revealed to His holy apostles (consecrated messengers) and prophets by the [Holy] Spirit.*
>
> Ephesians 3:3-5, AMP

The mystery concerning the Church is now revealed. Paul said,

> *(It is this:) that the Gentiles are now to be fellow heirs (with the Jews), members of the same body, and joint partakers (sharing) in the same divine promise in Christ through (their acceptance of) the glad tidings (the Gospel).*
>
> Ephesians 3:6, AMP

From eternity, God planned that the Gentiles and Jews would be made one Body...His Church...and that through Christ, not only would the Gentiles be received into the fellowship of the Saints, but they were in equal standing with Hebrew Christians.

We must never forget that the Church is not an accident or afterthought.

It is not just a structure that evolved because the Jewish people rejected Christ. Christians are not usurping the rights of God's Chosen people, the Jews.

From the beginning of time, God had a destiny for His Church.

He planned that the old dispensation under the old Covenant would be superseded by the new, and all those who accepted Christ, both Jew and Gentile, would be joined into one body, by His Spirit.

In this same chapter, Paul goes a step further in his unveiling of this great mystery to reveal God's purpose in keeping His great plan hidden throughout the ages. He explains the commission God gave him and then continues to reveal God's plan:

Paul said:

> ...*Also to enlighten all men and make plain to them what is the plan (regarding the Gentiles and providing for the salvation of all men,) of the mystery kept hidden though the ages and concealed until now in (the mind of) God who created all things by Christ Jesus. (The purpose is) that through the church the complicated, many-sided wisdom of God in all its infinite variety and innumerable aspects might now be made known to the angelic rulers and authorities (principalities and powers) in the heavenly sphere. This is in accordance with the terms of the eternal and timeless purpose which he has realized and carried into effect, in (the person of) Jesus Christ our Lord.*

Ephesians 3:9-11, AMP

By direct revelation, God unveiled the divine mystery to Paul so that He would make it known to the Church. God's purpose was that the Church throughout the succeeding ages, until Christ's return would be the instrument through whom He would reveal and manifest His plan to the world and the angelic principalities. Paul said,

> *(The purpose is) that through the Church the complicated, many-sided wisdom of God in all its infinite variety and innumerable aspects might now be made known to angelic rulers and authorities (principalities and powers) in the heavenly sphere*

Ephesians 3:10 AMP

Paul told the Ephesians:

> *And God raised us up with Christ and seated us with him in the heavenly realms in Christ Jesus, in order that in the coming ages he might show the incomparable riches of his grace, expressed in his kindness to us in Christ Jesus.*

Ephesians 2:6-7 NIV

God's Destiny For The Church Is Full Maturity

God's destiny for the Church is that we manifest to the world, and the Angelic principalities, the fullness of all that He has provided for us through Christ...salvation, healing, deliverance, overcoming power, strength, authority, and dominion. The Angelic principalities are watching...waiting to see the great end-time plan of God for His Church revealed through us!

God's destiny for the Church is that it grow and develop until it reaches full maturity, which is nothing less than the full stature of Jesus Christ. Paul said,

> *His intention was the perfecting and the full equipping of the saints (His consecrated people), (that they should do) the work of ministering toward building up Christ's body (the church), (that it might develop) until we all attain oneness in the faith and in the comprehension of the [full and accurate] knowledge of the Son of God; that (we might arrive) at really mature manhood [the completeness of personality which is nothing less than the standardheight of Christ's own perfection] he measure of the stature of the fullness of the Christ, and thecompleteness found in Him.*

Ephesians 4:12-13, AMP

- God's destiny for you is that you be perfected and fully equipped!

- His destiny for you is that you grow unto full maturity, to the full stature of Jesus Christ!

- It is His destiny that you be empowered to do the work of the ministry and build up the Body of Christ!

- His destiny for the Church is that we attain oneness in the faith and comprehension of the full knowledge of Christ!

Are you ready to step into your end-time destiny? God had this eternal destiny for the Church in his heart when He called Abraham out of his country and said, "*And I will make of thee a great nation...*" (Genesis 12:2).

When God spoke to Moses and chose the nation of Israel to be His people, He knew He would one day raise up a people, of every tribe and tongue, Jew and Gentile, who would be joined together as one body...His Church. God promised Moses,

> *And I will take you to me for a people, and I will be to you a God: and ye shall know that I am the Lord your God, which bringeth you out from under the burdens of the Egyptians.*
>
> Exodus 6:7

Today, under the new covenant, we are God's chosen people! Peter said,

> *But ye are a chosen generation, a royal priesthood, an holy nation, a peculiar people; that ye should shew forth the praises of him who hath called you out of darkness into his marvelous light...*
>
> 1 Peter 2:9

We are the people Hosea prophesied, who at one time were not God's people but are now called by His Name. Paul told the believers in Rome,

> *As he says in Hosea: I will call them 'my people' who are not my people; and I will call her 'my loved one' who is not my loved one, and, 'It will happen that in the very place where it was said to them, 'You are not my people,' they will be called 'sons of the living God.'*
>
> Romans 9:25-26, NIV

God's destiny for His Church has been revealed!
We are now God's chosen people!
We are His saints...His chosen set apart ones!
We are sons and daughters of the living God!
We are joint-heirs with Christ!
We are "a chosen generation"...chosen in Him before the world was formed!

We are the Body of Christ, purchased and washed by the precious blood of Jesus!

We are God's spiritual Israel!

God Has A Destiny For Israel

As we look closely at God's relationship with the nation of Israel and the purposes He desired to accomplish in and through their lives, we will understand more fully the end-time destiny God has for His Church in this end-time harvest.

From among the nations of the earth, God chose Israel. He made Himself known to them through great signs and wonders when He delivered them out of Egypt with a strong and mighty arm.

He brought them out of Egypt to Mount Sinai where He came down and met with them face to face. He revealed Himself to them in His great power as He ascended upon Mount Sinai in smoke and great flashes of fire.

God entered into a covenant relationship with Israel. In this relationship all that God had belonged to them. He became to them all that they needed or would ever need.

He became an enemy to their enemies.

The children of Israel became His people.

He established His covenant with them. He set them apart as His very own prized possession.

He established them as a holy nation...as kings and priests upon the earth.

He gave them specific promises as an inheritance.

God promised Israel:

1. To be an enemy to their enemies
   (Deuteronomy 28:7)

2. To drive out their enemies before them
   (Deuteronomy 11:23,25)

3. To bless their daily provisions
(Deuteronomy 28:8)

4. To take away sickness from them
(Deuteronomy 7:15)

5. None would miscarry nor be barren
(Deuteronomy 7:14)

6. To prolong their days upon the earth
(Deuteronomy 6:2)

7. To give them a land flowing with milk and
honey...the entire country between the Red
Sea and the Mediterranean on the one end
and the desert and the Euphrates on the other.
(Deuteronomy 11:24)

God made the children of Israel INVINCIBLE! Although they were greatly outnumbered, they were the most powerful people on earth. As long as they were obedient to Him, God drove out their enemies and made them victorious in battle. No man was able to stand before them!

> *And the Lord gave them rest round about, according to all that He sware unto their fathers: and there stood not a man of all their enemies before them; the Lord delivered all their enemies into their hand.*

> Joshua 21:44

God made them a strong and mighty nation. He multiplied and blessed them above the nations of their enemies.

He established them as a holy people.

God poured out His promised blessings upon them and they enjoyed an abundance of food, silver, and gold, livestock, houses, and land. God has not forgotten Israel. In this end-time hour He will fulfill all that He has promised.

God Has An End-time Destiny For His Church!

Today we are God's people, chosen and called by His Name. He has established us as a holy people! He has redeemed and delivered us out of Satan's bondage. We are no longer *"...strangers and foreigners, but fellow citizens with the saints and of the household of God"* (Ephesians 2:19).

God Almighty has placed His Spirit within us and we are His sons and daughters. By His Spirit we are One with Christ and one with Him!

God sent Christ to destroy the works of the devil and to pay the supreme price for us to live in total, 100 percent victory over 100 percent of the enemy's power, 100 percent of the time.

Do you think for one moment that God will do any less for the Church of Jesus Christ than He did for the nation of Israel?

NO!

Just as God made His people Israel the most powerful people upon earth, God planned for the Church to be invincible and immovable! He has placed within us His unlimited, immeasurable power that enables us to triumph in victory in every circumstance and overcome every attack of the enemy. Jesus said, *"...I will build my church, and the gates of hell shall not prevail against it!"* (Matthew 16:18)

Through Christ we have power and authority over all the power of the enemy. Through the Holy Spirit living within us we have the same power and anointing as Jesus flowing through us to heal the sick, cast out devils, and raise the dead!

There is NO POWER...NO FORCE...in earth or in hell that can defeat or destroy us!

Just as God blessed and prospered His people, Israel, we have power and authority in the Name of Jesus to ...ask anything in His Name and it will be done (John 14:13-14).

As Abraham's seed and Joint-heirs of the kingdom of God, we have inherited all the promises made to Israel.

Just as God transferred the wealth of the nations and gave Israel the "spoils" of the treasures of their enemies, God will in this end-time hour, transfer the wealth of this world into the hands of His people to fulfill His will in this end-time harvest! *"...a sinner's wealth is stored up for the righteous"* (Proverbs 13:22, NIV).

It is God that gives you power to get wealth.

God has not planned for the Church to know any limits. He has promised to supply all our needs *"according to His Glorious riches in Christ Jesus"* (Philippians 4:19, NIV).

He has promised to do *"...exceeding abundantly above all that we ask or think"* (Ephesians 3:20).

Jesus said,

> *And whatsoever ye shall ask in my name, that will I do, that the Father may be glorified in the Son, If ye shall ask any thing in my name, I will do it.*
>
> John 14:13-14

We can live in divine health and claim healing in Jesus' Name. He has already taken the stripes upon His back for our healing.

> *But He was wounded for our transgressions, He was bruised for our iniquities, the chastisement of our peace was upon Him; and with His stripes we are healed.*
>
> Isaiah 53:5

As His children we have access to all that God has and is! Through faith in Him and His Word we can take hold of His promises to receive all that we need!

We Are Destined To Be A Full Manifestation Of Christ To The World!

God never intended for His Church to know any limits!

Yet, a great majority of Christians are living far below their privileges as a child of God and what God has planned and made full provision to supply.

From eternity, God destined the Church to be a full manifestation of Christ to the world and to draw from Him everything we need. He cherished this plan and kept it hidden...a mystery until the time He determined.

His prophets gave glimpses of it through the prophecies He spoke through them. Christ came to earth, destroyed the works of the devil, paid the price to redeem and purchase the Church and sent the Holy Spirit to live and remain within us.

At the appointed time, God unveiled the mystery to the Apostle Paul and anointed Him to reveal it to the Church.

God plans for His Church today to manifest all that God has provided for us through Christ.

> *...In accordance with His good pleasure (His merciful intention) which He had previously purposed and set forth in Him, (He planned) for the maturity of the times and the climax of the ages to unify all things and head them up and consummate them in Christ, (both) things in heaven and things on earth.*
>
> Ephesians 1:9-10, AMP

We have a divine appointment with destiny!

Now in the fullness of God's time, He plans for the Church to reach full maturity where individually and corporately the Church is manifesting Christ in all His fullness...His power...His authority...His wisdom...His anointing...His glory.

Is it really possible?

Not only is it possible, this is part of God's destiny for His Church.

He has placed within the Church a divine capability, an unlimited power, which will bring it to a position of full maturity in this end-time hour.

Are you ready to step into God's end-time destiny for the Church?

Timing is the key!

The destiny of the Church was conceived, born and carried in the heart of God until He unveiled it to the Apostle Paul by direct revelation. If we limit our understanding regarding God's ultimate intention for the Church by our natural understanding, or according to the experience of the Church today, we will be unable to fulfill our spiritual destiny.

We must have a fresh revelation, direct from the heart of God by His Spirit!

Open your Spirit now to what God is saying to His Church and respond in faith. Allow God to take you beyond your natural limitations. Refuse to become satisfied with less than what God has revealed in His Word He has planned for you.

Receive a fresh revelation of God's destiny for the Church and for you!

CHAPTER FOUR

The Church...
A Supernatural, Indestructible
Superstructure!

Regardless of who you are or where you live...

Regardless of your nationality, your sex, or your age...

If you have been born again by the Spirit of God...

You are part of the most powerful force upon the face of this earth!

You are part of the Church...the Body of Christ...which cannot and will not ever be defeated nor destroyed!

The Church of Jesus Christ is of divine origin. The Church did not come into being simply as a result of the Apostles gathering believers together, nor through any human effort.

It was born through a supernatural impartation of the very life of Almighty God. And it is supernaturally empowered by the divine, life-giving flow of the Holy Spirit ...the Third Person of the Trinity!

When Jesus ascended into heaven, He placed gifts within the Church for the specific purpose of bringing it to a position of power whereby it is functioning in the same power as Himself.

> ...*When he ascended up on high, he led captivity captive, and gave gifts unto men...And he gave some, apostles; and some, prophets; and some, evangelists; and some, pastors and teachers; For the perfecting of the saints, for the work of the ministry, for the edifying of the body of Christ.*

> Ephesians 4:8, 11-12

He placed within the Church the supernatural "dunamis" miracle power of God (Acts 2:1-4), He sent the Holy Spirit, the Comforter, to dwell in us (John 4:16-17). And through the indwelling of the Holy Spirit, the Church has been given supernatural gifts of the Spirit which enable the Church to be a full manifestation of Christ to the world (I Corinthians 12:7-11).

Christ intends His Church to operate today in the fullness of His power in the same powerful dimension as He did while He was upon the earth.

He intends His Church to proclaim the Gospel in a demonstration of the Spirit and power with signs following.

He intends His Church to heal the sick, cast out devils and set the oppressed free.

In His plan for His Church there is absolutely no provision for weakness, failure or defeat!

Jesus said unto Peter: *"...upon this rock I will build my church; and the gates of hell shall not prevail against it"* (Matthew 16:18).

Christ is the Master Designer!

He is the Builder!

He is the Foundation!

He is the Cornerstone!

He is the Savior and Sustainer!

He is the Head!

Christ is building His Church, not man!

He is bringing together a holy people, possessing His power and glory, who will be a full manifestation of Himself to the world.

There is absolutely no power on earth or in hell that can ever defeat or destroy this Church Christ is building!

The atomic bombs or nuclear warheads are not the most powerful force on earth today.

The world's great political powers...the United States... China...Japan...are not the most powerful forces on earth today.

Communism is not the most powerful force on earth today.

Sin, sickness, and death are not the most powerful forces on earth today.

The evil powers and principalities with all their strongholds within the world today are not the most powerful forces. Satan and all his demons combined cannot stand against the Church of Jesus Christ. Jesus said of the Church: *The gates of hell shall not prevail against it!* (Matthew 16:18).

The most powerful force on earth today is the true Church...the Body of Christ!

The Church Is A Supernatural Organism!

Jesus conquered all the forces of hell and is now, at this very moment, seated in a position of supreme power and authority at the right hand of the Father as the divine Head of the Church:

> *...far above all principality, and power, and might, and dominion, and every name that is named, not only in this world, but also in that which is to come: And hath put all things under his feet, and gave him to be the head over all things to the church, which is his body, the fullness of him that filleth all in all.*
>
> Ephesians 1:21-23

As Head, He has given His Church His power and authority and established it to be the ruling force upon the earth. Jesus told Peter:

> *...thou art Peter, and upon this rock I will build my church; and the gates of hell shall not prevail against it. And I will give unto thee the keys of the kingdom of heaven: and whatsoever thou shalt bind on earth shall be bound in heaven: and whatsoever thou shalt loose on earth shall be loosed in heaven.*
>
> Matthew 16:18-19

Jesus delegated His power and authority to His Church. He gave us all power and authority to rule upon the earth. He gave us authority to bind...to declare unlawful...those things which have already been declared unlawful in heaven, and gave us the ability to loose...declare lawful...those things which have already been declared lawful in heaven.

The Church of Jesus Christ is not just a building on the corner. It is not simply a gathering of people on Sundays. It is not an organization controlled or governed by man.

The Church of Jesus Christ is a supernatural organism, supernaturally empowered and directed by the Holy Spirit, and Jesus said: *"...the gates of hell shall not prevail against"* (Matthew 16:18).

You are not merely part of a local congregation or man-made organization. You are part of a supernatural structure that is built upon Jesus Christ. The Church is a living, breathing organism comprised of thousands upon thousands of believers all over the world.

It is not a mystical, ethereal, invisible concept or theory. It is a literal, living superstructure. An "organism" is defined as "a comprehensive, living system of intertwined parts."

As part of this living organism you are not independent, functioning solely on your own, according to your own will. You are vitally linked to other members and are to be mutually dependent upon them.

I pray that God will give you a new, full revelation of this powerful, supernatural, indestructible superstructure of which He has made you a part.

You Are Part Of God's Household!

At one time you were a stranger, alienated from God by your own sins. But, when you were born again by the Spirit of God, God welcomed you as a member of His "household." Look at what the Apostle Paul told the Church in Ephesus:

> *Therefore you are no longer outsiders (exiles, migrants and aliens, excluded from the rights of citizens), but you now share citizenship with the saints (God's own people, consecrated and set apart for Himself) and you belong to God's (own) household.*

> Ephesians 2:19 AMP

You have been 'adopted' by His Spirit and are now part of God's Household.

Contrary to what you may believe, you did not become a member of the Church of Jesus Christ by simply joining a local church assembly.

You are not just a member of the Assembly of God, Lutheran, Baptist, Methodist, Presbyterian, Episcopal, or some other denominational church.

When you were born again by His Spirit, God Himself placed you within this supernatural organism called the Church. Paul told the Corinthians: "*But now hath God set the members every one of them in the body, as it hath pleased him"* (1 Corinthians 12:18).

No. You do not simply belong to a local church of a particular denomination.

You are part of a powerful, supernatural, indestructible superstructure, and the gates of hell shall not prevail against you!

The Church Is Built Upon An Indestructible Foundation!

The Church of Jesus Christ is not being built upon man-made ideas, doctrines or traditions. It is being built upon the foundation of the apostles and prophets. Paul said: *"...you are built upon the foundation of the apostles and prophets with Christ Jesus Himself the chief cornerstone"* (Ephesians 2:20, AMP).

Notice the Apostle Paul did not say the apostles and prophets were the foundation.

The apostles and prophets through their preaching and teaching, were builders who laid the foundation of the Church upon Jesus Christ. Jesus Christ Himself is the foundation.

Paul told the Corinthians:

> *...According to the grace of God which is given unto me, as a wise masterbuilder, I have laid the foundation, and another buildeth thereon. But let every man take heed how he buildeth thereupon. For other foundation can no man lay than that is laid, which is Jesus Christ.*
>
> 1 Corinthians 3:10-11

There is no other foundation! There is no other name given among men whereby men can be saved (Acts 4:12).

Throughout the ages, there have been those who have tried to build the Church upon great men and their teaching.

Even in the Church today there is a tendency to exalt great teachers and leaders. There are many Christians who are building their lives upon men's teachings instead of the Gospel of Jesus Christ.

The Church will not be built upon the power of positive thinking, upon man-made formulas for success and prosperity, nor upon any other message than the life, death and resurrection power of Jesus Christ. All other foundations which men try to lay will crumble and fall!

God, Himself, laid the foundation for His Church. God spoke through Isaiah concerning the foundation He was laying:

> *...Behold, I am laying in Zion, for a foundation a Stone, a tested Stone, a precious Cornerstone of sure foundation; he who believes (trusts in, relies on and adheres to that Stone) will not be ashamed or give way or make haste (in sudden panic).*
>
> Isaiah 28:16, AMP

The all powerful Church of the living God is being built upon a sure and strong foundation that is absolutely indestructible, which God Almighty has laid.

That sure foundation is Jesus Christ.

Jesus was a "tested Stone." He was tried, thoroughly tested and proven to be a strong and sure Foundation. He is the stone which was rejected and instead became a stumbling block to the Jews. But He became the Cornerstone. Paul said concerning Christ: *"This is the stone which was set at nought of you builders, which is become the head of the corner"* (Acts 4:11).

God sent Jesus to earth to give His life as a sacrifice for the sins of the world. Through His obedience unto death, He became the *"author of eternal salvation unto all them that obey him"* (Hebrews 5:9).

The Foundation for the Church was laid. Through His blood, Jesus cleansed us from our sins and separated us unto Himself as a holy people...a royal priesthood.

He purchased the Church with His own blood. He gave Himself...laid down His life willingly... suffered the agonizing death and humiliation of the cross...to cleanse the Church so that it would be holy and blameless before Him.

Paul told the Ephesians:

> *Husbands, love your wives, even as Christ also loved*

the Church, and gave himself for it; That he might sanctify and cleanse it with the washing of water by the word, That he might present it to himself a glorious church, not having spot, or wrinkle, or any such thing; but that it should be holy and without blemish.

Ephesians 5:25-27

The Church Jesus Christ is coming back to claim is a holy Church, without spot or wrinkle, not one who has compromised and played the harlot with the world.

Jesus is the rock of our salvation. He is the strong and sure foundation upon which the Church stands today. Regardless of what we face upon the earth, trials, temptations, testing, persecution, and even death...we know that we shall not be moved and the gates of hell shall not prevail against us!

With Christ as your foundation, your mind, will, and emotions centered and rooted in Him...you are also indestructible! When trials and circumstances seem to overwhelm you, you can cling to that Rock...that foundation which cannot be moved...and know that you will not fall.

We Are Joined Together With Christ Into A Powerful Superstructure!

The Church is not only being built upon Christ, a sure and strong foundation, which cannot be shaken or destroyed, we are supernaturally joined to Him by the Spirit. Paul said:

For we are members of his body, of his flesh, and of his bones.

Ephesians 5:30

The Church is not a lifeless, forma,l man-made structure. We are vitally united to Christ...members of His Body. We are part of Him...bone of His bone and flesh of His flesh!

We are joined together with Him into one body by His Spirit. Paul said:

69

*There is one body, and one Spirit, even as ye are
called in one hope of your calling; One Lord, one faith,
one baptism, One God and Father of all, who is above
all, and through all, and in you all.*

Ephesians 4:4-6

Paul told the Corinthians:

*For by one Spirit are we all baptized into one body,
whether we be Jews or Gentiles, whether we be bond or
free; and have been all made to drink of one Spirit.*

1 Corinthians 12:13

The Church of the living God is not only being built
upon Christ as a sure and strong foundation which cannot
be destroyed, it is also being bound and knit together with
Christ, who is the chief Cornerstone.

Paul told the Ephesian believers:

*You are built upon the foundation of the apostles
and prophets with Christ Jesus Himself the chief
Cornerstone. In Him the whole structure is joined (bound,
welded) together harmoniously; and it continues to rise
(grow, increase) into a holy temple in the Lord [a
sanctuary dedicated, consecrated and sacred to the
presence of the Lord].*

Ephesians 2:20-21, AMP

The word "cornerstone" literally means "at the tip of the
angle." It is the capstone or binding stone that joins and
holds the entire structure together.

In the East, the cornerstone was considered the most
important stone of the entire building. Its chief function is
to join together all stones within the building. It determines
the placement of the other stones. All the stones are aligned
with it. Without it, the building cannot stand.

Paul compared the Church with a building that is being built with Jesus as the chief cornerstone. Members of the Church are placed within the building as "lively stones." Peter told the believers:

And coming to Him as to a living stone, rejected by men, but choice and precious in the sight of God, you also, as living stones, are being built up as a spiritual house for a holy priesthood, to offer up spiritual sacrifices acceptable to God through Jesus Christ.

1 Peter 2:4-5, NAS

Both Paul and Peter had a clear vision of the Church of Jesus Christ. They saw true believers, God's consecrated, separated people being joined and fitted together with Christ the foundation and the cornerstone, into one powerful superstructure...continually growing into a holy temple in which God Almighty dwelt!

Look at Ephesians, 2:21-22 in the Amplified version:

In Him the whole structure is joined (bound, welded) together harmoniously; and it continues to rise (grow, increase) into a holy temple in the Lord [a sanctuary dedicated, consecrated and sacred to the presence of the Lord.] In Him [and in fellowship with one another] you yourselves also are being built up (into this structure) with the rest, to form a fixed abode (dwelling place) of God in (by, through) the Spirit.

You Are Part Of God's Holy Temple!

God will not dwell in an unholy temple, and the purpose of God in using you as part of His building is to form a place where He can dwell, where He can live, move, act and perform His divine will and purpose.

The Greek word used for "temple" here in this verse is "naos," which refers to the inner shrine. The central building of the temple was not a place of meeting or of worship. It was the Holy of Holies where God's Presence dwelt.

The true Church of Jesus Christ is not composed of the entire "visible" Church we see today with all those who attend our churches. Many of our churches today are filled with those professing and claiming to be members of the Body of Christ when they are not. They have made a profession of their faith and joined a local church, but they have not been truly born again and do not have a vital relationship with Christ. They continue to live their lives, fulfilling the lusts of the flesh, instead of walking in the Spirit.

Men have tried to build the Church with their own limited understanding and in their own limited strength. They have built churches based upon theology, the doctrines of men, and upon good moral standards. What they've been building is a natural structure, a denomination, not the true Body. As a result, they have produced churches which are no more than social institutions. They have built an outward shell, but have failed to reproduce the life of God.

In the midst of the hypocrisy, church politics, and spiritual apathy that is prevalent today in the Church, God is raising up a people. Supernaturally, by the power of the Holy Spirit, the true Church of Jesus Christ is being built with "living stones"...members of the Body...who are vitally joined together with Christ.

From every nation, every tribe and every tongue...

From every walk of life...

From every church denomination...

Christ is calling, separating, and consecrating a holy people and placing them in this powerful, indestructible, superstructure called the Church.

He is joining them together, and in this end time harvest, will bring them into full maturity, where they are united in the Spirit and living and manifesting the fullness of His power!

Christ is building His Church and the gates of hell shall not prevail against it!

Are you beginning to catch a glimpse of the glorious, triumphant Church of Jesus Christ of which you are now a vital part?

The Church, which was born in power, was a dynamic force marching from city to city, country to country.

Persecution came.

Disciples were beaten and stoned, imprisoned, beheaded, thrown to the lions.

Yet, on and on they marched, united in purpose, their eyes set upon one goal.

No force on earth or in hell has been able to stop God's Church!

Two thousand years have passed and it still marches on.

It has passed through periods of compromise, apathy, reform, and spiritual renewal.

It has been continually under attack from Satan, who has attempted to dilute its message, detour the saints from their task, and stunt its growth through fear and ignorance of God's Word. But God has preserved it and raised up a remnant for this end-time hour!

What Has Happened To The Church?

Today the Church has become sluggish and sleepy. It has been "marking time" for many years.

The power of God has not changed...the Church has changed.

Our eyes have been diverted.

Our unity has been broken.

Our fervor and zeal is diminished.

We are now living in the time God planned for His Church to rise up...to manifest Christ's glory and power to the world as a final end-time witness. This is our destiny!

However, before this can happen, something must happen to the Church that will bring us to the position of power God intended.

Before the Church can step into its end-time destiny, we must receive a new revelation of the power and glory Christ has given to the Church.

We need God to shake us out of our complacency!

We need a fresh outpouring of His Spirit to come upon us so that we will begin to walk in a full manifestation of His power.

What has happened to the Church of Jesus Christ?

What has happened to the living, moving body of believers that was born in an explosion of spiritual power?

What has happened to the Church Jesus said the gates of hell would not prevail against?

What has happened to the spiritual kingdom Jesus established, that Daniel prophesied one day would take dominion over the earth?

> *And in the days of these things shall the God of heaven set up a kingdom, which shall never be destroyed: and the kingdom shall not be left to other people, but it shall break in pieces and consume all these kingdoms, and it shall stand forever.*
>
> Daniel 2:44

There are many things that have happened over the centuries that have caused the Church to reach such a weakened condition. Satan, the arch deceiver, has deceived generation after generation into thinking that he is in control of the earth...that there is nothing that can be done about the sin, sickness, or death that plagues our world today.

One of the major reasons why the Church has not become the ruling force on the earth God intended it to be is because...

The church lost the vision of what God intended it to be!

God never intended the unlimited, immeasurable power of the Holy Spirit to be limited nor contained within the four walls of what we call churches today!

He never intended the Church to be fragmented, split by denominationalism, or man-made philosophies or traditions. NEVER!

God never intended the Church to know any limits!

The Church experienced its greatest growth during the first three centuries. The Church of Jesus Christ literally exploded and was able to evangelize the entire world without the aid of large sanctuaries and cathedrals... without the aid of organized programs... without the aid of modern technology!

The disciples weren't afraid to let go of the old rituals, the old forms of worship and formalism of the past, and allow the Holy Spirit to effect radical changes in their lives. They didn't place limits upon the power of God flowing through them, but positioned themselves spiritually where the Holy Spirit could flow through them unhindered.

Are You Ready To Step Into God's End-Time Destiny For His Church?

God has been preparing the Church. Now, He is releasing a fresh anointing of the Holy Spirit that calls for radical changes in our lives, in our way of thinking, in our way of living, in our way of ministering and fulfilling His purposes.

Are you ready to draw a line on your past...to let go of the old form and traditions that are holding you back from experiencing the fullness of the power of God flowing in your life?

Are you really hungry for Christ to release a full manifestation of His power in your life?

God wants to give you a new anointing of His Spirit. You cannot live off the old anointing. It was sufficient for yesterday's challenges, but not for today. He wants to set your life on fire with the true power of Pentecost that will enable you to demonstrate and manifest the resurrection power of Jesus Christ to the world!

Get ready for changes to happen within you and within your ministry. Be pliable in the hands of God, and allow Him to do whatever is necessary...to cut away the things holding you back...to purge and cleanse you of anything that would block the flow of His power and anointing through you.

The cry of my heart today is:

"Oh God, take the scales from our eyes. Enlarge our spiritual vision. Increase our knowledge. Perform Your work through us. Purge out the dead works and the dead formalism.

"Breathe new life...new revelation...new faith ...new power. Pour out a new anointing on us. Baptize us with power from on high! Lift up those who are weary and discouraged. Awaken those who are sleeping.

"Unite us as one. Reveal Your glory in us and through us. Speak through us...pour out Your love through us...heal and deliver through us. Glorify and fill Your Church with Your abiding Presence. In Jesus' Name. Amen and Amen!"

If this is the desire of your heart, take time right now, before you go any further in this book, to fall to your knees in prayer.

Allow God's Presence to fill the room you are in. Ask Him to help you see the unlimited power He has placed within His Church and within you.

Ask God to help you see the Church today as the powerful, supernatural superstructure He intended it to be and what He wants to accomplish in your life in this end-time harvest.

The Church has a unique end-time destiny. Before the foundation of the earth, God planned to raise up a mighty people who are fully equipped, fully empowered and who are manifesting His power and glory to the world.

God's ultimate intention for us extends far beyond the redemption and salvation of our souls. Christ's finished work on the cross and our deliverance from sin is just the beginning...the first step toward what God has planned to accomplish in and through us.

God desired to have a people...sons and daughters...who would bear His image, His nature, His purpose, His vision, and be fully conformed to His will!

This is your spiritual destiny and mine.

By His Spirit, God is bringing us into a new phase of full spiritual maturity. He is bringing to pass and fulfilling His ultimate intention for the Church.

Are you ready to step into God's end-time destiny for His Church?

Paul exhorted believers in the Early Church:

> *Therefore, let us go on and get past the elementary stage in the teachings and doctrine of Christ (the Messiah), advancing steadily toward the completeness and perfection that belongs to spiritual maturity.*

Hebrews 6:1, AMP

It's time to press forward!

It's time to forget the past and lay aside every distraction!

Focus your vision and press forward in hot pursuit to obtain all that God has planned for you.

CHAPTER FIVE

"...Wait For The Promise..."

The one hundred and twenty disciples gathered together in Jerusalem had a **divine appointment with destiny!**

Before the foundation of the earth, God planned to raise up a people unto Himself in whom His power and glory would be manifested.

He planned the day He would enter into a covenant with His chosen people, Israel, on Mount Sinai. And, He planned the day He would raise up a new people, enter into a new covenant with them and place within them His Spirit.

God promised through His prophets:

> *A new heart also will I give you, and a new spirit will I put within you: and I will take away the stony heart out of your flesh, and I will give you an heart of flesh. And I will put my spirit within you, and cause you to walk in my statutes, and ye shall keep my judgments, and do them.*
>
> Ezekiel 36:26-27

He promised:

> *...and they shall be my people, and I will be their God.*
>
> Ezekiel 11:20

He promised through the prophet Joel that He would pour out His Spirit upon all flesh:

> *And it shall come to pass afterward, that I will pour out my spirit upon all flesh; and your sons and your daughters shall prophesy, your old men shall dream dreams, your young men shall see visions: and also upon the servants and upon the handmaids in those days will I pour out my spirit.*
>
> Joel 2:28-29

The Children of Israel had a divine appointment with destiny.

At the time appointed by God, fifty days after the first Passover, when He had supernaturally delivered the children of Israel out of Egyptian bondage, God came down and met with them on Mount Sinai.

On that day, as they were assembled together, God manifested His powerful presence in fire and billowing smoke. He met with them there and entered into a covenant with them and they received the law.

The quietness of the early morning was shattered with mighty roars of thunder! Lightning flashed through the sky.

Mount Sinai shook violently as the Great I AM...God Almighty...descended upon it in flaming fire.

The entire mountain was covered as the smoke billowed up from it like a huge furnace. The people trembled in fear as the trumpet of God blasted across the plain, summoning them together at the foot of the mountain. Then, out of the midst of the fire, God spoke audibly to them.

That day the Nation of Israel was born. The children of Israel became God's people and He became their God.

For hundreds of years the Israelites celebrated Pentecost...fifty days after the firstfruits offering...in remembrance of that day when God established His covenant with them on Mount Sinai.

More than 1,400 years later, at the time divinely appointed by God...fifty days after Christ's resurrection...He sent the mighty outpouring of His Spirit, giving birth to the Church of Jesus Christ!

God again came down in a mighty demonstration of power...in the rushing wind and tongues of fire...and entered into a New Covenant with His people.

These disciples had gathered together in obedience to Christ's command to wait in Jerusalem for the promise of the Father.

And, being assembled together with them, commanded them that they should not depart from Jerusalem, but wait for the promise of the Father, which, saith he, ye have heard of me. For John truly baptized with water; but ye shall be baptized with the Holy Ghost not many days hence.

Acts 1:4-5

Jesus told them:

...behold, I send the promise of my Father upon you: but tarry ye in the city of Jerusalem, until ye be endued with power from on high.

Luke 24:49

Jesus told them to *"wait for the promise of the Father..."* This was one of the most important instructions Jesus gave them before He ascended into heaven.

These disciples were ordinary men and women. They were humble fishermen. Matthew was a tax collector. Among the 120 were Jesus' brothers, Mary, the mother of Jesus, and other women who had followed Jesus. Mary, the woman out of whom Christ had cast seven devils, and Lazarus whom Christ had raised from the dead, were probably there among the 120.

They were basically uneducated. They didn't have any formal training. They hadn't been to a theological seminary. They weren't great orators. Yet before He ascended to heaven, Christ called and commissioned them to preach the Gospel to the ends of the earth! (Mark 16:15)

These same men and women had followed Jesus during his three and one-half years of ministry. They talked with Him. They ate with Him. They sat and listened to Him teach. They watched as He ministered to the great needs of the people. Over and over again they saw Him open the eyes of the blind, heal the deaf and lame, heal all manner of sickness and diseases, cast out devils and raise the dead.

Yet, when the Roman soldiers came to arrest Jesus in the Garden of Gethsemane, they all betrayed Him and ran in fear. Standing outside Pilate's judgment hall, Peter denied Him three times.

They hid behind closed doors. The women went to the tomb to anoint a dead body. Not one of the disciples had believed in His resurrection. Even after the women had seen Jesus after His resurrection and told the disciples, they still did not believe.

Jesus commanded them to wait...to wait for the promise of the Father...to wait until they had an experience of power.

In their own limited strength and wisdom, they were incapable of fulfilling the awesome responsibility Christ had given them. The future of the Church and the work of God were resting upon them. If something didn't happen to them, there wouldn't be a Church...the work of God would not be accomplished.

In essence, Jesus was saying, "You're not ready yet! Wait in Jerusalem until you have an experience of power. Don't you dare leave the city until you are *'endued with power from on high.'*"

Jesus Knew The Disciples Weren't Ready

Jesus didn't tell them to wait until they received the gift of tongues, the "prayer language" of the Holy Spirit, or some other manifestation of the Spirit. He told them to wait until they were endued with power. The word "endued" means "clothed".

Jesus said, "Go, wait for the promise of the Father." What promise was He talking about? The promise He had spoken of through His prophets of the outpouring of God's Spirit!

Jesus said, "I'm going to send the promise of the Father upon you, and you're going to be endued...clothed with power from on high. You're not going to have to depend upon your own strength any longer...you're going to be clothed with God's dunamis power."

It's not going to be manifested occasionally, at certain times in your lives. Like a garment placed upon you that you wear, God's dunamis power will come upon you and remain in you!

He told them, "You're going to be baptized with the Holy Ghost! The Holy Ghost will come upon you and manifest Himself in your life until you are saturated... controlled...directed and empowered!"

Jesus knew these disciples were not ready...that before they would be able to fulfill the commission He had given them, they needed an experience...a power encounter with Almighty God!

God knew that...if these followers of His Son were to be able to fulfill the Divine Commission they would need a supernatural power.

These 120 disciples were ordinary men and women, just like you and me. They were only human vessels with their weaknesses, failures, and shortcomings.

Something had to happen within their lives that would transform them from a fearful, weak, doubting group of men and women...without a vision, without a purpose or direction...into bold, fearless men and women, full of faith and the power of Almighty God, capable of shaking the entire world!

They had a divine appointment with destiny!

You and I, as part of the true Church of Jesus Christ, also have a divine appointment with destiny. God is not looking at your weaknesses and failures. He is not depending upon your natural talents and abilities to accomplish His will in this end-time harvest.

Aren't you glad God is not depending upon who you are or what you possess to stand against Satan's forces, and accomplish the work He has given us of reaching the world with its unreached masses who have never heard the Name of Jesus?

Whether you are a doctor, lawyer, computer technician, teacher, carpenter or housewife, God is not depending upon any natural abilities you possess just as He was not depending upon anything the disciples possessed.

Jesus said, *"Wait for the promise of the Father."* During His final moments with them before the crucifixion, He had told them how the Holy Spirit...the Comforter...the Spirit of truth...would not only come, but would live in them.

Jesus said:

> *If ye love me, keep my commandments. And I will pray the Father and he shall give you another Comforter, that he may abide with you forever; Even the Spirit of truth; whom the world cannot receive, because it seeth him not, neither knoweth him: but ye know him; for he dwelleth with you and shall be in you.*

> John 14:15-17

Jesus told them that when the Holy Spirit...the Spirit of Truth...had come, He would testify of Him:

> *But when the Comforter is come, whom I will send unto you from the Father, even the Spirit of truth, which proceedeth from the Father, he shall testify of me.*

> John 15:26

He knew that their hearts were filled with sorrow and that they were fearful and discouraged because He had told them He was returning to the Father. But, He knew that if He did not die on the cross, rise from the dead and ascend back to the Father, the Holy Spirit would not come.

He had told them:

...It is expedient for you that I go away: for if I go not away, the Comforter will not come unto you; but if I depart, I will send him unto you. And when he is come, he will reprove the world of sin, and of righteousness, and of judgment.

John 16:7-8

In Simple Obedience...They Waited!

Before He ascended into heaven Jesus told them they would be "baptized" with the Holy Ghost.

The disciples believed, received and acted on the promise. They went into the upper room in Jerusalem and assembled there together with one mind and one accord.

They shut out everything else, laid aside their businesses, their own personal needs, their fears, and their concerns regarding the future. They had determined that they were going to wait until they had been baptized with the Holy Spirit and experienced the power Christ promised they would receive.

Day after day they waited.

The air was charged with a sense of expectancy. They didn't know what was going to happen or when. They didn't have any preconceived ideas about how the Holy Spirit was going to come; nor were they looking for any particular type of manifestation.

They came together in faith, in simple obedience to Christ's command, trusting and believing that they would be baptized in the Holy Spirit, as He had promised. They did not waste their time and energy on unimportant issues, but focused all their attention upon receiving from God this promised blessing.

Each day as they gathered together, they waited in the presence of God through prayer and supplication. They were not asking or begging for the Holy Spirit to be poured out upon them. Christ had already told them He was sending the Holy Spirit to live within them. They were coming into God's presence...seeking ...longing...crying out for Him to manifest His power in their midst.

They did not offer up occasional half-hearted prayers. They were continuously in prayer.

> *These all continued with one accord in prayer and supplication, with the women, and Mary the mother of Jesus, and with his brethren.*
>
> Acts 1:14

They had a divine appointment with destiny!

They were not waiting for just a temporary manifestation of God's power, but for the Holy Spirit to enter into a relationship with them, whereby He would live within them.

In this relationship with the Holy Spirit, He would...

• Convict of sin! (John 16:1, 8-11)

• Regenerate! (John 3:3;5)

• Sanctify! (Romans 15:16)

• Anoint! (I John 2:20, 27)

• Empower! (Acts 1:8)

• Guide! (John 16:3)

• Comfort! (John 14:16-26)

• Impart gifts! (I Corinthians 12:3-11)

• Bear fruit! (Galatians 5:22-23)

• Illuminate their minds! (Ephesians 1:16-17)

• Teach! (John 14:26)

• Testify of Christ! (John 15:26)

• Transform! (2 Corinthians 3:18)

The 120 were waiting for the Holy Spirit...the Third Person of the Trinity...to be sent from the Father, who would live and remain within them. Jesus told them they would be baptized with the Holy Ghost.

The word "baptism", is translated from the original Greek word *baptismo*, meaning to immerse or submerge." It is used in Scripture to describe the spiritual experience where Christ baptizes an individual with the Holy Spirit.

Jesus is the Baptizer. He is the One who sent the Holy Spirit. John the Baptist said when Jesus came He would "baptize" them with the Holy Ghost and fire (Matthew 3:11-12). Jesus said, "When the Holy Spirit comes upon you...when you're "baptized"... you will receive power!

> *But ye shall receive power, after that the Holy Ghost is come upon you: and ye shall be witnesses unto me both in Jerusalem, and in all Judea, and in Samaria, and unto the uttermost part of the earth.*
>
> Acts 1:8

There is a vast difference between being "filled" with the Spirit and being "baptized" with the Spirit. One of the reasons why we see so little of the true power of Pentecost manifested is because the majority of Christians have not yet had a revelation concerning what it really means to be baptized with the Holy Spirit. They have stopped at the point of blessing!

Jesus did not tell them to wait until they had received the gift of tongues. He told them to wait until they were endued... clothed with the dunamis power of God from on high!

In those final moments, before He ascended into heaven, when Jesus said, "But ye shall receive power..." He was not just speaking words. He was imparting the power and authority to the Church!

He was not just speaking at that moment to His disciples. He was speaking to the Church...to you and me today, two thousand years later! At that moment, He was imparting the power and anointing of the Holy Spirit through His promise to us.

God Breathed His Spirit Upon Them Giving Birth To The Church!

At the time divinely appointed and determined by God, He breathed upon the disciples gathered in the upper room and gave birth to the Church of Jesus Christ!

On the tenth day...fifty days after Christ had risen from the dead...when the day of Pentecost had fully come ...they were assembled together, waiting for the fulfillment of the Promise.

The doors were shut. The air was charged with a sense of expectancy.

Suddenly they heard a sound as a rushing mighty wind sweep into the room. It was not an earthly sound. It was a supernatural sound from heaven. God breathed upon them!

From the throne room of Almighty God, the Holy Spirit was sent forth!

God breathed His life...the same resurrection power that raised Christ from the dead...into the one hundred and twenty disciples.

God breathed the Holy Spirit into them. They were baptized...immersed...submerged...infused throughout their beings with the Holy Spirit.

What they received that day was an infusion of power. They were anointed with the same power of the Holy Spirit that was upon Jesus.

God anointed Jesus of Nazareth with the Holy Ghost and with power...

Acts 10:38

Just as God anointed Jesus with the Holy Ghost and with power, He anointed the one hundred and twenty in the upper room.

The tongues of fire which appeared above their heads were a visible manifestation that they had been baptized with the Holy Spirit. It was a sign that the Holy Spirit had come to live within them, giving them power from on high!

As the tongues rested upon them, the Holy Spirit was at work, cutting away their "stony hearts of flesh"...bringing their entire beings...their minds, wills, spirits...back into unity with God.

The fire of God represents His purifying power...the refining fires of the Holy Spirit. Their hearts were being circumcised *"with a circumcision not made with hands"* (Colossians 2:11). He was cutting away their selfishness, their doubts, their wrong attitudes and the things that divided them.

God had breathed upon them. Through the Spirit taking up residence within them, they became one with God and one with each other!

God Gave Birth To A Church Without Limitation!

In the divine destiny of God, the Church was born through a mighty demonstration of power. God gave birth to a Church without limitation!

He never intended the Church to be limited!

He never intended the power and anointing that was released at Pentecost to decrease!

Contrary to what many believe, the outpouring of God's Spirit...the manifestations of His power...the manifold gifts of the Spirit...did not cease to function with the Early Church.

God did not send forth the Third Person of the Trinity, the Holy Spirit, in a demonstration and manifestation of power so that this Church would be weak, anemic, powerless, and under the enemy's power.

The Church was born in power and God has planned for it to operate today in a full manifestation of that same power!

The Day of Pentecost marked a new era for God's people and the world.

The old was fading away, and God was ushering in the new...pouring out the new wine of the Holy Spirit.

With the coming of the Holy Spirit, man was able to enter a brand new relationship with God, whereby His very life and presence would dwell within man, reproducing God's life and giving him divine capability to overcome all the power of Satan, and to fulfill His will upon earth.

With the outpouring of the Holy Spirit and power, God raised up a new breed of people, a people walking in His power and authority to fulfill His will.

The one hundred and twenty emerged transformed from fearful, unbelieving, cowering, wavering disciples who had hidden behind closed doors, to fearless men and women who boldly declared the Gospel of Jesus Christ in a demonstration of power with signs following.

No longer were they full of doubt, confused, or fearful. They had an experience of power...they possessed a divine capability to do the same work Jesus had done.

Peter, who had denied Christ three times at His crucifixion for fear of the Jews, now full of the power of the Holy Ghost, stood to his feet and boldly declared to the multitude who had assembled:

> *...these are not drunken, as ye suppose, seeing it is but the third hour of the day. But this is that which was spoken by the prophet Joel.*
>
> Acts 2:15-16

Peter identified what had taken place as being the fulfillment of God's promise through Joel of the outpouring of His Spirit. There was no question or doubt in his mind. He said, "This is it! This is the promise of the Father...the outpouring of His Spirit."

The Disciples Possessed A Divine Capability

With this mighty outpouring of God's Spirit, not only was the Church of Jesus Christ born in power, the disciples walked in power. Everywhere they went, they preached the Word in a demonstration of power!

The message Peter preached that day was with power. He did not give them a long theological dissertation. He did not try to impress them with his knowledge of the Scriptures. He preached Jesus Christ, crucified, resurrected, and seated in power and glory at the right hand of the Father.

Three thousand souls who heard and saw the manifestation of God's power were baptized and added to the Church that same day.

As the power of God flowed throughout the Apostles and believers in the church, God multiplied their numbers.

And fear came upon every soul: and many wonders and signs were done by the apostles.

Acts 2:43

...And the Lord added to the church daily such as should be saved.

Acts 2:47

The next thing we read about is Peter and John on the way to the Temple. As they are walking they see a beggar, a lame man lying on the ground. He was carried daily to the gate of the Temple to beg alms of those passing by. No doubt, Peter and John and the other disciples had passed him by before on their way to the Temple. But, that day as they passed by this man it was different. They were no longer the same men.

They were full of the Holy Ghost and power! They had a divine capability they never had before. They had a new boldness and a greater understanding of God's purpose for their lives.

When Peter saw the lame man lying at the gate of the temple, he did not hesitate. I do not believe he stopped to consider what he should do. I believe the power of God was so strong within him that it was a natural outflow of the Spirit that caused him to reach out, take the man by the hand and command him in the Name of Jesus to rise up and walk.

Could it be that the lack of this 20th Century Church ministry lies in the weakness of our relationship with the Lord and in the Spirit?

As Peter spoke the word of healing in the power and authority of the Name of Jesus, and lifted the man to his feet, the dunamis miracle power was released, and immediately the man was healed. He began leaping and walking, and entered into the temple, praising God!

This miracle of healing in Jesus' Name provided undeniable proof that Jesus is who He claims to be, the Son of the Living God. No one could deny it. The man stood before the people as living proof. As Peter preached under the anointing of the Holy Spirit, 5,000 were added to the Church!

There was such an awesome flow of God through Peter that the people brought the sick into the streets and laid them on beds and couches so that as he passed by his shadow would fall on the people and they would be healed.

Insomuch that they brought forth the sick into the streets, and laid them on beds and couches, that at the least the shadow of Peter passing by might overshadow some of them.

Acts 5:15

There was a divine flow of God's power through Paul. They took cloths, which had been placed upon Paul's body, and placed them on the sick as a point of contact. The power of God was released and the sick were healed and demons cast out!

> *And God wrought special miracles by the hands of Paul: So that from his body were brought unto the sick handkershiefs or aprons, and the deseases departed from them, and the evil spirits went out of them.*

Acts 19:11-12

This power was not limited to just the Apostles. Jesus promised:

> *And these signs shall follow them that believe; In my name shall they cast out devils; they shall speak with new tongues...They shall lay hands on the sick, and they shall recover.*

Mark 16:17-18

Everywhere they went they preached the word in a demonstration of power. Signs and wonders were manifested! Multitudes were added to the Church! The sick were healed and devils cast out!

Something Must Happen To The Church!

The purpose of the outpouring of the Holy Spirit which began on the Day of Pentecost has not changed!

The power of the Holy Spirit was given to the Church to proclaim the Gospel of Jesus Christ with signs and wonders as evidence that Jesus is the Son of God.

Paul told the Corinthians:

> *For the kingdom of God is not in word, but in power."*

1 Corinthians 4:20

93

It wasn't the preaching. It wasn't their natural speaking abilities or powers of persuasion. It wasn't their personalities that enabled the disciples in the Early Church to evangelize the known world. It was the power of the Holy Spirit flowing through them.

Paul told the believers in Thessalonica:

...For our gospel came not to you in word only, but also in power, and in the Holy Ghost...

1 Thessalonians 1-5

He told the Corinthian Church:

...my speech and my preaching was not with enticing words of man's wisdom, but in demonstration of the Spirit and of power: That your faith should not stand in the wisdom of men, but in the power of God."

1 Corinthians 2:4-5

In essence Paul was saying, "I'm coming to you with a very special ingredient. When I get there, this anointing, this power will give me the ability to manifest and demonstrate the resurrection power! The blind will see! The deaf will hear! The lame will walk!"

Something happened to the disciples. When the Holy Spirit came to dwell within them, they were changed! It was more than a celebration...more than just speaking in unknown tongues...more than an emotional experience... more than laughing, more than being slain in the Spirit, or any other outward manifestation.

The one thing that distinguishes the Church today from the Early Church is that they had a full demonstration and manifestation of the power of the Holy Spirit flowing through it, and today we don't.

Without the same enduement of power...this same demonstration of God's power...there is no hope for this world!

Something must happen to the Church!

During the first three centuries, the Church experienced its greatest growth. But something happened in the third century that hindered and blocked the flow of God's power. We will look at some of these hindrances and see God's plan for His end-time Church.

From the third century until the present time, in the twentieth century, we have not seen that same powerful demonstration of the true power of Pentecost with signs, wonders, and miracles being manifested.

One of the major reasons why the Church today no longer has the full manifestation of power, as it did during the first two centuries, is because through the centuries, man placed limitations upon God and the working of the Spirit.

Men tried to confine the power of God within a structure based upon their natural, limited understanding; their man-made traditions and ideologies.

Our faith has been in what man can produce... man's wisdom...man's abilities...man's technologies... instead of the power of God. We have become too dependent upon ourselves to get the job done of evangelizing the world.

The old "wineskins" of the Church structure have placed limitations upon the free-moving of the Holy Spirit calling for radical change.

Men have tried to confine the moving and working of the Holy Spirit to their narrow concept and limited understanding of how the Holy Spirit should operate within the Church.

Over the years, the Church has quenched or tried to restrict the moving of the Holy Spirit. But, God is ready to do a new work within the Church. The old "wineskins" of the

Church structure, which have been binding and hindering the flow and demonstration of the power of God, is going to prepare the way to the new!

One of the major changes God showed me would be taking place in the decade of the 90's was within the structure of the organized Church. God is going to break man's traditional barriers that are hindering the Church from operating as He intended. Many Christians, including pastors and Christian leaders, are going to find it very difficult to accept and cope with these changes.

As the Spirit of God begins to break through the traditional structure of the Church, a separation is coming. Pastors, Christian leaders, and laymen who are bound by their traditions, man-made doctrines, and the structure of their denominations will be unwilling to accept these changes, and will remain part of the dead, dry, structure of the Church. They will not recognize these changes as the move of God and will resist them.

God has an end-time destiny for His Church!

He never intended the power and anointing of the Holy Spirit that was released at Pentecost to diminish. He never intended His miracle-working power, or the gifts of the Spirit to cease functioning within the Church.

God Never Intended His Church To Know Any Limits!

There is not one Scripture that reveals God ever planned the Church to be weak, defeated, to be limited, or to fail to produce the same power that was manifested on Pentecost. Not one!

God raised up the Church for a divine purpose. He raised up the Jews and manifested His supernatural power in their lives through signs, wonders and miracles as a witness to show the world that Jehovah, is the great "I AM." He raised up the Church, placed His supernatural miracle-working power within it as a witness to the world that Jesus is Who He claims to be, the Son of the Living God!

This is probably the most awesome prophecy God has given me!

A new wave of Pentecostal power will sweep over those who want to be part of God's end-time plan. God has been waiting to literally pour this out.

There is coming an awesome manifestation...a divine capability will once again be given to God's people...to show the world that Jesus Christ is the all-powerful Son of the Living God, and that there is salvation, healing, and deliverance in His Name!

God hasn't planned to put any limitations upon the release of His power through you!

God has destined you to be a man or woman of power and authority through whom He manifests His supernatural power in healing the sick, casting out devils, raising the dead, and fulfilling His will in this end-time hour!

Get yourself positioned!

God is about to unveil a greater power and glory than the Church has ever known.

Consider The Experience Of The Church Today.

Where is the power that once flowed through the Apostolic Church?

Within the Church there are ministers, pastors, and entire denominations who deny the very power that gave birth to the Church. They believe the supernatural gifts of the Spirit, the working of miracles and healing were given only to establish the Church, but they are no longer necessary and have ceased to function.

For hundreds of years, the Church has been blinded from seeing the truth by man-made doctrines and theories. Men have taught that miracles are carnal, they are no longer necessary, and that God no longer works through miracles.

These are lies straight from the pit of hell and have hindered the Church from being the powerful force God intended it to be.

Within the Church, we have treated the preaching and the working of miracles as two separate aspects of ministry. There are very few churches where the Word is being preached with miracles accompanying the Word. Miracles have become the exception rather than the normal function of the Church.

How did the Church get so far away from God's original purpose for the ministry of the Church?

Jesus empowered and equipped the Church so we would be able to set people free from the bondage of Satan, to loose them from their infirmities, and meet the desperate needs in their lives. He infused the Church with the power of the Holy Spirit so that we would be able to carry on the same ministry He had upon earth.

Through the power of the Holy Spirit operating in our lives, Christ intends for us to do the same works He did and greater! Jesus said:

> *...He that believeth on me, the works that I do shall he do also and greater works than these shall he do; because I go unto my Father. And whatsoever ye shall ask in my name, that will I do, that the Father may be glorified in the Son.*
>
> John 14:12-13

Miracles did not cease with the early Church! God has always had a remnant of people through whom He can manifest His power and glory to the world. Throughout the years, God has raised up men and women...ordinary people like you and me...and baptized them with the Holy Spirit, giving them power and authority to work miracles in the Name of Jesus.

God called me as a young, 14 year-old, Jewish orphan boy; baptized me with the Holy Spirit, and sent me around the world preaching the Word with signs following. Throughout the more than 56 years of my ministry, God has supernaturally manifested Himself in bringing multiplied thousands of souls into the Kingdom of God, healing the blind, opening deaf ears, and supernatural healings of all types of sickness and disease. I have seen blind eyes opened! I have seen many cripples get up out of wheelchairs, rise off the ground — healed by the power of God. Demons have been cast out in Jesus' Name.

Through the years, God has raised up and anointed men and women with great ministries of healing and deliverance. He has used them mightily in manifesting miracles throughout the nations of the world. However, He did not intend only a few select individuals to manifest His supernatural power, which has been the case.

God has an end-time destiny for His Church!

God planned the entire Body of Christ...especially His end-time people...to be infused with His power and authority to manifest miracles in His Name.

God has placed within every believer, through the power of the Holy Spirit, the same divine capability to do the same miraculous works of Jesus, in His Name. He has called and chosen you to be a living witness, to give visible proof, that Jesus is the Son of God.

Don't you dare listen to Satan's lies that you are just an insignificant person, and that you cannot do the same miraculous works that Jesus did!

Don't you dare cast aside the power and authority Jesus has given you in His Name!

We are a people of spiritual destiny!

In these final moments of time before Christ's coming, He has given us an awesome responsibility. The Gospel is to be preached throughout the nations of the earth before Christ returns.

Jesus said:

> *And this gospel of the kingdom shall be preached in all the world for a witness unto all nations; and then shall the end come.*
>
> Matthew 24:14

The world is going to have a final end-time witness of the power of the Gospel of Jesus Christ...not just the preaching of the written word...but the resurrection message of Jesus Christ will be preached in a demonstration of the supernatural power of God with accompanying miracles as living proof that Jesus is Who He claims to be...the Son of the Living God!

In John's vision of the end times, he saw an angel flying through the heavens with the Gospel to preach to the nations of the earth (Revelation 14:6).

This angel preaching the Gospel represents an end-time move of world evangelization that will take place before Christ's return. This end-time world evangelism will not only be accomplished by mass evangelistic crusades or through the preaching of well-known evangelists alone.

We are going to see technological breakthroughs and new opportunities through satellite technology that will enable us to go into areas never before reached by the Gospel, and we will be able to multiply the number of people that we reach many times over.

However, this is not the major method that will be used to get the job done. We are entering a new era of evangelism, where the work will be accomplished through one-on-one evangelism.

The true Body of Christ will be empowered to do the work of the ministry...not just the well-known evangelists, pastors, teachers, and ministers from behind the pulpit, but the members of the Body will go forward with a new authority and a new boldness...one on one, house to house, on the job, at the market place...everywhere they go until the whole world is covered with the Gospel.

The Church Is Going To Grow To Full Maturity!

The Word will be preached by the Body of Christ in a demonstration of God's miracle-working power:

The blind will see!

The lame will walk!

Demons will be cast out!

The Word of God will increase and bring forth a multitude of souls around the world!

God will use the Body of Christ, a holy end-time remnant, to manifest His power and bring salvation and deliverance to the world as a final witness before his return. He is pouring out His Spirit upon us for this specific purpose.

He is going to have a people who are going forth in His power confronting the power of Satan and setting those who are bound by sin and sickness free.

He is going to have a people who are living witnesses... visible, undeniable proof...that Jesus is the Son of God by the miracle-working power flowing out of their lives!

The Body of Christ will rise up in the power and anointing of the Holy Spirit to proclaim the Gospel of Jesus Christ.

We will not be preaching a watered-down compromising message to tickle people's ears. We will be preaching the message of Jesus Christ in a demonstration of the supernatural power of Almighty God.

We will not just be talking about God's miracle power to save, heal, deliver from drugs, alcohol, and all the power of the enemy. God will be confirming what we say with signs following.

The members of the Early Church went from house to house in one-on-one evangelism daily!

> *And daily in the temple, and in every house, they ceased not to teach and preach Jesus Christ.*
>
> Acts 5:42

The Holy Spirit was gushing forth into their lives and they couldn't stop!

When they were persecuted and scattered abroad, they did not stop! Everywhere the believers went, they were spreading the Gospel!

> *Therefore they that were scattered abroad went every where preaching the word.*
>
> Acts 8:4

God Has Destined You To Be An End-time Witness!

As God's people of destiny, we cannot accomplish the tremendous task God has given us of evangelizing the world in our own limited strength. With all our computer and space-age technology, we cannot do it. We cannot do it using man-made strategies or church programs.

The world is going to have a final end-time witness through a manifestation of the supernatural power of God that He is the one true and living God.

Just as He manifested Himself in signs and wonders on behalf of Israel...

Just as He confirmed the Word with signs following in the Early Church...

God will confirm the Word through His end-time Church with His mighty power!

This is God's end-time destiny for His Church.

Are you ready to take your position and step into your end-time destiny?

God has destined you to be an end-time witness to the world.

Are you ready for the true power of Pentecost to be manifested in and through you?

You may be thinking, "I am not a preacher. I'm not a public speaker. I'm just an insignificant person. I don't have any special talents or abilities. How can God possibly use me to proclaim the Gospel in a demonstration of power?"

Please...don't place limitations on the power God has placed within you through the Holy Spirit or what He can accomplish through you!

God used a handful of ordinary men and women... fishermen...tentmakers...a tax collector...and the most unlikely individuals...to evangelize the world. He took them with all their limitations and all their shortcomings, and poured His Spirit into them, giving them power to evangelize the entire world!

God will take you with all your human weaknesses and shortcomings and transform you until His power is flowing unhindered through you.

Remember, God is not depending upon your abilities or anything you possess.

By His power which is working within you, He will give you the divine capability to proclaim the Gospel with evidence...undeniable proof!

Jesus told the disciples "...wait for the promise of the Father..." He told them He was sending the promise of the Father upon them, but they were to wait until they were *"endued with power from on high"* (Luke 24:49).

Jesus said:

> *But ye shall receive power, after that the Holy Ghost is come upon you: and ye shall be witnesses...*
>
> Acts 1:8

This is Christ's promise to you.
Receive it.
Believe it.
Act on it!
You have a divine appointment with destiny!

You are a candidate to have the same power of the Holy Spirit manifested in your life that was flowing through Peter, Paul and the other disciples...the same power of the Holy Spirit that flowed through Jesus!

Present yourself to the Lord in seasons of prayer. "Wait" upon Him in faith...as the 120 disciples did...in full expectation of the fulfillment of this promise in your life.

Ask God to "baptize" you with the Holy Spirit as He did the disciples on the Day of Pentecost. Even if you are already "filled" with the Spirit, ask the Lord to submerge you in His Spirit until you are saturated, directed and controlled by His Spirit. Don't be satisfied or settle for anything less!

Rid yourself of all preconceived ideas regarding any outward manifestations and yield yourself fully to Him. Then, walk in His power...let it flow out of you to heal the sick, proclaim deliverance, and set the captives free.

Your destiny is to be an end-time witness to the world of Christ and His resurrection power. When He said, "you will be my witness," what type of witness does He expect you to be? What kind of witness are you giving to the world?

CHAPTER SIX

Witnesses!

Knowing that we are a people of destiny, and that God planned to fulfill His divine purposes in and through His Church in this end-time hour, we must refocus our attention and efforts upon being all He has destined us to be, and completing all that God has called and anointed us to do.

Throughout the ages, the Church became sidetracked and diverted from the original purpose God intended it to fulfill. Instead of being the indestructible powerful force God intended and a full manifestation of Christ to the world, it became splintered...divided by denominationalism and bound by man-made traditions and doctrines.

The major focus of the Church turned inward. Instead of focusing upon ministering to the desperate needs of the world around us in a demonstration of the power and anointing of the Holy Spirit, we have placed our major focus upon building large sanctuaries and buildings, filling them with people, and ministering to the needs of the believers inside the Church.

The vast majority of Christians within the Church today have become satisfied and are content just warming a church pew. The average Christian has a very limited vision for the lost within his community, and an even more limited vision and burden for multiplied millions of lost souls around the world.

When God gave birth to the Church He never intended the ministry of the Church to remain within the four walls of what we call the Church today. God didn't send forth the Holy Spirit...the blessed Third Person of the Trinity...and release His immeasurable, unlimited power within the Church just so the Church would be able to soak up God's blessings, speak in tongues, shout, dance, and sing the praises of God while thousands are dying daily... going into an eternity without God...forever damned in the pits of hell.

When God breathed His life and power into the Church, He intended every believer to proclaim the message of salvation, healing and deliverance, and meet the desperate needs of the world in a demonstration of power!

The power that was released in Jerusalem on the Day of Pentecost has not diminished! It has not stopped flowing within the Church. This is the key. We must understand...because when you look at the denominations and the structure that is to represent the church, you can have every right to question the absence of the manifestation of the power of Pentecost.

The Church is not the denominations we see today as a whole.

The Church is not the physical structure of the buildings we see today.

The Church is Christ's Body. It is the representation of what God is-it is His people- of every walk, race, color, creed, and denomination.

Each of us knows the sense of what is in us that unite us to each other-the spiritual, mystical cord that has deep calling unto deep.

That same dunamis, miracle-working power that was manifested in Jesus' life, and was demonstrated in the Early Church to heal the sick, open blind eyes, make the lame walk, and to raise the dead, is still flowing today within the Body of Christ.

Pentecost did not end two thousand years ago. It never stopped!

Within the Body of Christ there has been a lack of understanding concerning the true power that was released at Pentecost and its purpose within the Body of Christ. This is one of the major reasons why we are not seeing more of God's miracle power manifested within our churches.

One of the biggest lies Satan will use to block the flow of the fullness of God's power through your life is to tell you that it's impossible for the miracle power of God to flow through you as it did through Peter, Paul, and the disciples in the Early Church. He will try to make you think God's miracle power is released only through great "spiritual giants"...well-known evangelists, ministers, or teachers.

Remember, God's power is not limited by who you are or by your own limited talents and abilities. His power is not dependent upon you.

God will manifest that same miracle power through you as you begin to understand the power He has already given you through the Holy Spirit. Then, as you dare to step out in faith and expect Him to release that power to heal the sick, cast out devils and proclaim deliverance in His Name, He will do it!

What Is God's Destiny For His End-Time Church?

What is God's end-time destiny for you!

There would be absolutely no need for God to give us the promise of power if it were not for service and ministry.

Jesus came to earth for a divine purpose. He said, *"My meat is to do the will of him that sent me, and to finish his work"* (John 4:34).

It's time for the Church to wake up and to grow up! We must completely refocus on fulfilling the will of God in this end-time hour. Jesus said, "I didn't come to do my will but I came to do the will of my father."

The manifestation and power of the Holy Spirit is to give us the ability to accomplish His purposes. The power of the Holy Spirit was given to equip the Church and give us the ability to fulfill the great commission.

God knew we could not do it in ourselves. That is why He sent the Holy Spirit with power to remain in us! We cannot accomplish the will of God in our own limited strength and natural abilities. There is no way that we can take our lives and lay them on the altar as a one hundred percent sacrifice. No way!

We must have an experience, a personal, divine encounter with God...where He implants His Spirit within us, giving us the power and ability to completely submit and yield ourselves to Him in obedience to His will.

We must have a relationship where Christ is continually revealing Himself to us by His Spirit. Only as we truly know Him intimately will we know His purpose for our lives.

What is God's destiny for His Church today in this end-time harvest?

What is God's destiny for your life?

To answer these questions, let us go to the mountainside near Jerusalem where Christ met with His disciples and gave them His final parting instructions. Five hundred of His disciples were gathered together for the most important meeting Jesus ever had with them.

They had a divine appointment with destiny.

The entire future of the Church rested upon how they responded to Christ's final directive.

This was Jesus' last day on earth.

The atmosphere was charged with emotion. Jesus was alive! After three days, He had risen from the dead just as He had promised! He had been with them forty days giving them undeniable proof of His resurrection.

This was one of the greatest days of victory ever known to mankind. Jesus had defeated Satan and all his principalities. He broke the power of death and freed man from his slavery to sin. He had fulfilled the purpose for which God had sent Him to earth.

...For this purpose the Son of God was manifested, that He might destroy the works of the devil.

1 John 3:8

He was the mighty Victor returning in great triumph and glory to His Father. Because of His willingness and obedience to God in laying down His life on the cross, He was highly exalted and given a Name above every other name in heaven and in earth. He was returning to the glory which He had with the Father, where He would be seated at the Father's right hand,

> ...*far above all principality, and power, and might, and dominion, and every name that is named, not only in this world, but also in that which is to come: And hath put all things under his feet, and gave him to be the head over all things to the church, which is his body, the fullness of him that filleth all in all.*

> Ephesians 1:21-23

In these final moments, Jesus was preparing His disciples to carry on the ministry He had begun in setting people free from the bondages of sin, sickness, and death. Although He would no longer be physically with them, through the indwelling of the Holy Spirit, He would live within them. He would manifest His power in their lives to fulfill His purposes.

Even after Jesus had revealed Himself to them and demonstrated the reality of the power of His resurrection, they still did not understand the significance of what He had called them to do. They were unable to spiritually discern that the hour God ordained for the Church had arrived. In a few short days they were going to be transformed and thrust into an unprecedented outpouring of God's Spirit that would give birth to the Church and forever impact all the peoples, tribes, and nations of the world. Yet, they could not comprehend what was happening.

Their understanding, before the Holy Spirit came, was limited. Their spiritual senses were dull. They were unable to grasp or comprehend many of the things Jesus had told them;

nor did they fully understand the Scriptures. There was no revelation because the Holy Spirit had not yet come. Jesus had told them, *"I have yet many things to say unto you, but ye cannot bear them now"* (John 16:12).

However, He promised to send the Comforter, Who would live within them and reveal all they needed to know. He promised:

> *Howbeit when he, the Spirit of truth, is come, he will guide you into all truth: for he shall not speak of himself; but whatsoever he shall hear, that shall he speak: and he will shew you things to come. He shall glorify me: for he shall receive of mine, and shall shew it unto you.*
>
> John 16:13-14

The Hour God Ordained For The Church Has Arrived!

In a previous meeting on a mountain in Galilee, Christ revealed to the disciples exactly what He had called them to do. He told them;

> *...All power is given unto me in heaven and in earth. Go ye therefore, and teach all nations, baptizing them in the name of the Father, and of the Son, and of the Holy Ghost: Teaching them to observe all things whatsoever I have commanded you: and, lo, I am with you always, even unto the end of the world.*
>
> Matthew 28:18-20

The message and commission were clear. As He was preparing to return to the Father, He was sending them forth in His Name to preach the glorious message that He was crucified, had risen from the dead and ascended into heaven, where He was seated at the right hand of the Father in a position of supreme power! He told them, *"...as my Father hath sent me, even so send I you"* (John 20:21).

Jesus was sending them forth to fulfill what seemed to be an impossible task. In the natural, it was impossible for a small handful of men to evangelize the world.

Now, in His final moments with them, He commanded them to wait in Jerusalem until they were *"endued with power from on high"* (Luke 24:49).

Jesus knew the disciples were not ready...that before they could be able to fulfill this commission, they needed an experience of power!

In essence, Jesus told them, "You get into Jerusalem, and don't you dare leave. You wait."

I call upon the Church to repent before God for the way in which we have characterized the blessed Third Person of the Trinity.

Jesus said, "You will receive power 'after' the Holy Ghost comes upon you." Don't think for a moment the Holy Ghost has entered the lives of so many people around you claiming to be Christians and claiming to be filled with the Holy Spirit.

God promised through the Prophet Joel that He would pour out His Spirit upon all flesh (Joel 2:28). But, He never said it would come until His people had an experience. It never comes without experience. It didn't come to Moses without his experience in the desert. And, it will never come until you have an experience.

Jesus told them, "Something is going to happen to you. You're going to be changed! You're going to be baptized with the Holy Ghost! In a few days the Holy Ghost is going to come upon you and manifest Himself in your life until you are saturated... controlled...directed, and empowered!

The doctrine regarding the baptism of the Holy Spirit is the most misunderstood doctrine in the Church today. The Apostle Paul told the Corinthians, "When I come to you,

Corinthians, I'm going to talk to you about a man named Jesus. I'm not coming with enticing words of man's wisdom, I'm coming to you in a demonstration of the Spirit and power of Almighty God!"

Paul was not an ignorant person. He was an intelligent man who studied at the feet of Gamaliel. He was a religious leader, a Pharisee of pharisees. He came from a well-educated family.

But, when you have an experience, something happens to you...you're changed! The world doesn't understand this. In fact, 90 percent of the church people do not understand this, because they have never experienced it! With the coming of the Holy Spirit, men are changed!

Jesus Refocused Their Attention Upon Their Destiny!

Are you ready to refocus your attention on God's end time destiny?

The disciples asked Jesus a very revealing question. The question was, "Was he now going to set up and restore the kingdom to Israel?"

This question reveals something very important to us about Jesus' disciples. They had heard what Jesus said but they were still concentrating on the natural. They were still thinking in terms of an earthly, physical Messiah. It seems almost as if they hadn't really learned anything.

They hadn't believed in His resurrection. They ran from the cross. They hid. They denied Him. Now, after He had been with them and had spent forty days manifesting infallible proofs that He was the resurrected Son of the living God, they still couldn't see past the natural, the physical, and the material things of this world.

They were totally absorbed with the natural. They said, "Lord, we're glad you're back. We're glad you're not in the grave. We're glad you're alive. We're ready! Now, are you going to restore the kingdom to Israel?"

Jesus rebuked the disciples for asking this. He said, "It's not for you to know. You've got your focus in the wrong direction. You've got your mind on an earthly kingdom. You forgot what I've taught you. You forget I told you the real, true purpose for which I came here."

If you want to go past the surface, past the natural, into a true experience of God's power, your focus and your concern is not on a "reward."

Your craving is not to be the recognition of man and prestige, rule and reign...the material and the physical.

There, on that hillside, Jesus refocused the attention of those five hundred believers and disciples away from the material...away from the world...away from the natural, and focused their attention upon the true purpose He intended them to fulfill.

The focus to which Jesus brought these five hundred upon this hillside, full circle around, and the true purpose of the Church today is to be on service and ministry.

The purpose of the power of the Holy Spirit is to give us the ability to proclaim the glorious salvation of Christ, and that we will be equipped to meet the cry of a world that is buried in desperate needs, waiting for someone who can manifest power!

The purpose of the manifestation of the Holy Spirit in our lives is to give us power to fulfill the Great Commission.

If it were not for that, we would never have needed the Holy Spirit's power!

What a scene! The disciples asked about the position of leadership. They asked Christ about the authority He had promised. We can't disregard it. They were to receive power, but it was not an earthly, natural power.

The power was to be spiritual.

It was to be supernatural.

The power was to be God Himself!

The power was to be the Supreme Being of the universe. The power was to be Him, Who created us in His own image.

The power was to be the very Presence of the Shekinah glory of God Himself! It was to be the very Spirit of God!

We have a God-given task. We have a mission to carry out on this earth. We don't have the power to carry out that mission. The power is of God Himself.

God Has Destined You To Be His Witness!

Christ told the disciples,

> *But ye shall receive power, after that the Holy Ghost has come upon you: and ye shall be witnesses unto me both in Jerusalem, and in all Judea, and in Samaria, and unto the uttermost part of the earth.*
>
> Acts 1:8

There are two major points in this verse which reveal the destiny God has planned for your life. These two major points are absolute. They are unquestionable! They are the result of being baptized with the Holy Spirit.

1. You will receive power!
2. You will be witnesses unto me!

The word "witness" used in this verse has a far deeper meaning than we understand today. To be a witness is much more than just simply "testifying" or proclaiming the Gospel of Jesus Christ to unbelievers.

Two thousand years ago when the disciples walked down the streets and declared to the unbelievers that Jesus was the Son of God and that He came from heaven, they had to do more than talk. They had to prove what they said about Him.

They were talking to people who had seen Jesus in the flesh. They saw Him get tired. They saw Him get hungry. They saw Him need to rest.

After they saw Him die on the cross...after He was buried, the disciples were walking the streets of Jerusalem telling the same people...that felt Him...handled Him, slept with Him, ate with Him...that He came from God. They were telling the world that when they put Him in the grave, "We are His witnesses...we saw Him. He is alive! The grave couldn't hold Him! Death couldn't keep Him! Chains couldn't imprison Him. Bars couldn't lock Him up...He tore them away...He arose!"

The word "witness" is translated form the Greek word "martus." So many "witnesses" laid down their lives for their testimony about Christ that the word "martyr" gradually became understood as "one who bears witness by his death." It was adopted into the English language as "martyr."

"Witness" (translated from this Greek word "martus") refers to "one who can or does verify or prove what he has seen, or heard, or knows."

The word "witness" means "to give or to be evidence: one who furnishes evidence, proof; one who demonstrates, substantiates, or verifies his testimony with an exhibition of evidence."

The last words Jesus spoke to His disciples were, "...ye shall receive power, after that the Holy Ghost is come upon you; and ye shall be witnesses unto me..." When He finished speaking, as the disciples fixed their eyes steadfastly upon Him, He ascended into Heaven and a cloud covered Him from their sight.

Within these final parting words of Jesus are the two things which sum up the spiritual destiny God planned for His Church.

1. We are to no longer function and live our lives according to a natural power, but according to a supernatural power that is imparted by the indwelling of the Holy Spirit.

2. As a result of this supernatural power flowing through our lives, we will be witnesses...giving proof and demonstrating the power of the resurrection and evidence that Jesus is Who He claims to be, the Son of the living God!

This is the destiny God has planned for your life and mine! It is for every believer who will dare to take Christ at His Word and act on His promise.

We are no longer bound to live our lives according to our natural power and abilities. God does not intend us to try to fulfill His work upon the earth in our natural strength. Jesus said, "You will receive power!" You will be witnesses unto me!"

The future of the Church was resting in the hands of these disciples and how they would react and respond to Christ's promise of this supernatural power, and His command to wait in Jerusalem until they were baptized with the Holy Spirit.

In essence Jesus was telling these disciples, "You're going to be My witnesses. I've been the witness. I've been showing the people I am Who I claim to be. I've been showing infallible proof that the grave could not hold me. Satan could not victimize me. Chains could not bind me. Prison doors could not enslave me. I arose!

"I'm going back to My Father and you are going to be witnesses unto Me. You're going to show the world I am not just another God, I am not just another so-called Messiah who died on the cross like others have died.

"You are going to give witness that I am Who I claim to be, not Mohammed, not Buddha, not Shinto. I am the Way. I am the Truth. I am the Life!"

Forty Days Jesus Bore Witness Of Himself

With this final promise burning like a fire within their hearts, the disciples returned in obedience to Jerusalem to wait.

At the time ordained by God, fifty days after Christ's resurrection, the 120 disciples gathered together in Jerusalem and were baptized with the Holy Spirit.

As a result, they became witnesses of Christ through the signs and wonders that followed:

> *And with great power gave the apostles witness of the resurrection of the Lord Jesus: and great grace was upon them all.*
>
> Acts 4:33

They were not "witnesses" simply by the words or message they preached. They demonstrated the power of God through their actions. Luke wrote, "And with great power gave the apostles witness!" The miracles God worked through them in the Name of Jesus were evidence of the resurrection power of God and that Jesus was the Son of the living God!

During the forty days Jesus was with His disciples before His ascension, He had prepared them for the tremendous work of establishing the Church that He was entrusting into their hands.

> *To them also He showed Himself alive after His passion (His suffering in the garden and on the cross), by (a series of) many convincing demonstrations (unquestionable evidence and infallible proofs), appearing to them during forty days, and talking (to them) about the things of the kingdom of God.*
>
> Acts 1:3 AMP

Jesus appeared to them and demonstrated the resurrection power of God so they would be eyewitnesses of His resurrection. These appearances were not just a probability or the figment of someone's imagination. Jesus gave them "infallible proofs." They were unquestionable...100 percent accurate, with no possibility of error!

During those forty days Jesus was giving witness. Forty days He showed Himself giving infallible proof. "I told you before I died on the cross, I will rise again. Believe! The chains of death could not bind me. My Father came from heaven and broke those chains from me. I opened the prison doors and I arose. I am alive! Believe!"

The undeniable proof of Jesus' resurrection from the dead was and is the foundational truth upon which the Gospel stands.

Without the resurrection, there would not have been a Day of Pentecost!

The Holy Spirit would not have been sent forth!

There would be no salvation...no life...no power!

Forty days Jesus showed Himself alive to His disciples by many infallible proofs!

The chains of death could not hold Him!

There was no power on earth or in hell that could keep Him in the grave!

His appearances demonstrated there is no greater power!

Resurrection day...the earth quakes...the stone is rolled away...the tomb is empty! Many saints rise from their graves and appear in Jerusalem...evidence...living proof of the resurrection (Matthew 27:52-53).

Jesus appears to Mary Magdalene as they were on their way to tell the disciples that the tomb was empty. He said, *"...Be not afraid: go tell my brethren that they go into Galilee, and there shall they see me"* (Matthew 28:10).

Undeniable proof!

Peter and John ran to the tomb. They saw the empty tomb and the linen cloth that had been wrapped around Christ's body, lying there (Luke 24:12).

Undeniable proof!

The same day Jesus appeared to two of His disciples on the road to Emmaus, which was a seven-mile walk from Jerusalem. They were discouraged, grief-stricken, despondent! They had heard the women's report that the grave was empty, Jesus was alive, but they still had not believed. Jesus rebuked them for their unbelief and began to explain to them all the Scriptures concerning Him. As they talked, their eyes were opened, they recognized Him before He vanished out of their sight (Luke 24:30-31).

Undeniable proof!

The same day he appeared to His eleven disciples and those gathered together with them. They had gathered behind closed doors because they were afraid of the Jews (John 20:19). They were perplexed and greatly disturbed ...confused...fearful.

All of them had forsaken Him. They had fled for their lives when He was taken to be crucified. Not one of the disciples had believed that He would rise from the grave.

Suddenly Jesus appeared in their midst and said, "Peace be unto you." But when they saw Him, they were so startled and terrified, they thought they had seen a spirit.

Jesus reproved them for their unbelief. He told them,

Look at my hands and my feet. It is I myself! Touch me and see; a ghost does not have flesh and bones, as you see I have.

Luke 24:39, NIV

He stretched out His arms and showed them His hands and feet. And when they still did not believe, He took a piece of fish and ate it.

The disciples saw His nail-pierced hands and feet. They touched Him. They saw him eat fish. He was alive!

Undeniable proof!

Eight days later, Jesus again appeared to His disciples. Thomas had not been with them when Jesus had appeared to them earlier. When the disciples told him they had seen Jesus, he doubted.

Again the doors were shut. Jesus appeared in their midst. *"Peace be unto you!"* He looked at Thomas and said, *"Put your finger here, see my hands. Reach out your hand and put it into my side. Stop doubting and believe"* (John 20:26-27, NIV).

Thomas reached out and felt the nailprints in Jesus' hands. He placed his hand in Jesus' side where it had been pierced by the Roman soldier's sword, and he knew and believed it was the Lord.

Undeniable proof!

On the sea of Galilee, Jesus appeared to Peter and six other disciples who had gone fishing. They had fished all night and caught nothing. Early in the morning, they saw Jesus standing on the shore, but did not realize who it was (John 21:3-6).

Jesus told them to cast their net on the right side of the ship. When they cast their net on the other side, there was such a miraculous catch of fish they were unable to haul the net in!

When they saw the miraculous catch of fish, and the fish He had prepared for them, they knew it was Jesus.

Undeniable proof!

The Disciples Were Living Witnesses Of God's Power!

Before He ascended into Heaven Jesus knew it was vital to give His disciples these infallible proofs.

The disciples were eyewitnesses of His life and resurrection and had been chosen to preach the message of repentance and forgiveness, in the Name of Jesus, to all nations, beginning in Jerusalem. As eyewitnesses of His resurrection it was their responsibility to prove to the world Jesus was the Son of God.

They were able to say we have seen Him... touched Him...talked with Him...eaten with Him. We saw Him ascend into Heaven!

After the Day of Pentecost when the Holy Spirit came upon them, they were witnesses of Christ-not through their own natural abilities, through their preaching or powers of persuasion, but they proved Jesus was Who He claimed to be through the supernatural power of God working signs and wonders through them. They demonstrated the power of His resurrection.

The true power of Pentecost is the power to be witnesses...to produce proof...to give evidence...to demonstrate to the world through the supernatural power of God flowing through us to heal the sick, cast out devils, and proclaim the Gospel with boldness.

Luke wrote, "And with great power gave the apostles witness!"

On the Day of Pentecost Peter began his message by declaring that this man Jesus, whom they had days before crucified, God had raised from the dead. The grave could not hold Him. He was alive forever more! He told them, *"This Jesus hath God raised up, whereof we all are witnesses"* (Acts 2:32).

The multitude, upon seeing and hearing the mighty manifestation of God's power...the rushing mighty wind...the one hundred and twenty declaring the mighty works of God in the languages of the Jews who had gathered around the world...and Peter's message delivered in the power and unction of the Holy Spirit, repented. Three thousand souls were baptized and added to the Church that same day!

When Peter said to the crippled beggar, *"In the Name of Jesus Christ of Nazareth rise up and walk"* and lifted him to his feet, he was bearing witness.

With the man who had been healed standing beside him, Peter began to boldly preach the message of Jesus

Christ to the multitude who had gathered together. He again focused his message upon the truth of Christ's resurrection from the dead. He told them, "...we are witnesses!" In essence, Peter was saying, "We are witnesses of His resurrection. We produce evidence! Here it is...this man standing before you is evidence. He has been healed through faith in Jesus' Name!"

When the rulers, elders and high priests, saw what had happened they laid hands on Peter and John and threw them into prison. The next day they gathered together, and brought Peter and John before them and demanded to know by what power or what name this great miracle had taken place (Acts 4:7).

Not only did Peter preach that Jesus had resurrected, and that He was the only way through which man could be saved, he was producing the proof...visible evidence...that Jesus had been resurrected from the dead and that there is healing power in His Name.

The Pharisees and High Priests saw the man who had been lame from his mother's womb forty years ...made 100 percent whole. They could not deny that a great miracle had been manifested, but they refused to believe in Christ because they were still bound by the old formalism and traditions of their religious dogma.

When Peter and John were commanded not to speak in the Name of Jesus, they didn't shrink from the conflict. They weren't intimidated. They laid hold of the dunamis power of God within them. They looked the High Priest and elders squarely in the face and said, ... *Whether it be right in the sight of God to hearken unto you more than unto God, judge ye. For we cannot but speak the things which we have seen and heard* (Acts 4:19-20).

The fire of Pentecost was burning in them!
There was not a trace of fear in them.
Something happened to them.

...And if we are to experience our divine appointment with destiny, it must happen to us.

The unlimited power of God was working within them, and it could not be quenched!

Jesus said, "You shall receive power! You shall be witnesses!"

God bore witness to them and the Gospel by the manifestation of His signs and wonders and with miracles, and gifts of the Holy Ghost, according to His will (Hebrews 2:4).

Peter was a living witness! The power of God flowed through him in such a measure that just his shadow falling upon the sick would heal them (Acts 5:15-16).

The whole region near Lydda was converted to Christ after Peter healed a man who had been paralyzed eight years.

A multitude in Joppa believed after Peter raised Dorcas from the dead (Acts 9:40-42).

In Samaria, multitudes believed when they saw and heard the miracles God manifested through Philip (Acts 8:5-6).

One man, full of the power of the Holy Spirit, preaching the Gospel in a demonstration of the miracle power of God, shook an entire city. When they heard and saw the miracles he did...the demons cast out...the lame walking...they believed the Word!

Christ appeared to Paul and called him to be a witness. He told Paul,

But rise, and stand upon thy feet: for I have appeared unto thee for this purpose, to make thee a minister and a witness both of these things which thou hast seen, and of those things in the which I will appear unto thee.

Acts 26:16

The power of God flowed through Paul in such a dimension that they took cloths which had been placed upon his body and placed them on the sick. Diseases were healed and demons cast out!

In Ephesus, Paul was a witness through his teaching and the miracles manifested through him. Ephesus became a center from which all of Asia was evangelized (Acts 19: 8-12).

Nothing Could Silence These Witnesses!

The disciples were witnesses!

But, this power was not just flowing through the Apostles, the power of God was flowing through the Church. The believers shared the Gospel of Jesus Christ everywhere they went...in their homes... house to house...in their places of work...in the streets...at the marketplace. They prayed for the sick, cast out devils, ministered to the needy and spread the Gospel throughout their cities.

When strong persecution broke out in Jerusalem against them, it was the saints who were dispersed and spread the Gospel to the nations, while the Apostles stayed in Jerusalem (Acts 8:1).

These believers did not run and hide for fear of persecution. Everywhere they went, they declared the Gospel. They were witnesses, not only by the words they spoke but by the signs and wonders God manifested through them.

Jesus said,

And these signs shall follow them that believe; In my name shall they cast out devils; they shall speak with new tongues; they shall take up serpents; and if they

*drink any deadly thing, it shall not hurt them; they shall
lay hands on the sick, and they shall recover.*

Mark 16:17-18

When opposition and persecution came against the
Church these witnesses could not be silenced. There has
never been a more deadly and longer persecution in the
history of mankind than the war that has raged against
Christians.

Christians were beaten, sold into slavery, tortured,
thrown to lions, crucified, burned at the stake, sawn asunder
for their witness of Jesus Christ. But nothing could defeat or
stop them.

As they laid down their lives, they were witnesses of the
power and truth of the Gospel. Every martyr was living
proof of the reality of the message they preached. The
persecution of the Church, which continued nearly 300
years, instead of destroying it, was the very thing God used
to mobilize and build the Church into an invincible power.

The believers' faith and endurance in the face of death
was a witness of His Presence among them.

These witnesses marched into the Roman
amphitheaters to face a cruel death in the jaws of the lions
with an unshakable faith that could not be quenched.

They were witnesses to the truth and reality of the
salvation hope of eternal life that was proclaimed in Christ.

No opposition, no persecution, no work of the enemy
could stop these witnesses.

God's End-Time Church Must Refocus
On Its True Purpose!

How do we translate what happened in the lives of
these witnesses two thousand years ago into the

experience of the Church today as the twentieth century is closing and we are entering the twenty-first century?

What is God's purpose for His end-time Church?

In light of the fact that we are the end-time generation and believe Christ is coming soon, what is the major focus we must have before Christ returns for His Church?

With all my heart I believe this is God's time to bring the Body of Christ into an experience of power that will shake the world before Jesus comes!

The Church is at a point of destiny!

God's purpose for this end-time Church is the same as it was for the believers in the early Church. The divine charge Jesus gave the disciples before He ascended into heaven has not changed.

We face the enormous task of reaching the world with the Gospel before Christ returns. With our population nearing six billion and multiplied millions upon millions who have not yet been reached with the Gospel, we must have a supernatural manifestation of the true power of Pentecost.

The future success of this twentieth century Church lies within the hands of those who will grasp hold of the two great truths Jesus declared...

"You will receive power!"

"You will be witnesses unto Me!"

Without the same enduement of power...the same demonstration of God's power that was released within the early Church...there is no hope for this world!

There is only one way that we will be able to evangelize the world before Jesus comes. We must have an experience of power, where we have been baptized...immersed...completely saturated...with the Holy Spirit so that we will be witnesses of the resurrection power of Jesus Christ to the world.

The true power of Pentecost was the power to proclaim the Gospel of Jesus Christ with evidence... by signs and wonders manifested through the disciples and believers.

This purpose has not changed.

We have Christ's promise, *"...ye shall receive power after that the Holy Ghost is come upon you; and ye shall be witnesses unto me..."*(Acts 1:8).

Through the Holy Spirit living within us, we have power to proclaim the Gospel in the same demonstration of power that was manifested in the early Church. Christ has equipped and empowered us. And it is the responsibility of every born again believer to accept this charge and fulfill it in the power of the Holy Spirit.

God is calling His end-time Church to refocus upon the purpose He has for us.

One of the most important end-time signs which Jesus said would occur before His return is that there will be an incredible end-time witness of the Gospel to the world. Jesus said, "This gospel of the kingdom shall be preached in all the world for a witness unto all nations; then shall the end come" (Matthew 24:14). This is the true purpose for the Holy Spirit being outpoured upon the Church today.

Just as the believers in the early Church were witnesses of Christ's resurrection through the signs and wonders which God manifested through them, God has called and chosen us to be His end-time witnesses...to produce proof through the miracles God has planned to manifest through us to meet the desperate needs within the world today.

The last thing Jesus did to prepare His disciples to fulfill the great commission was to refocus them upon their true purpose. Once they were focused and experienced the Holy Ghost, they never again looked to the world. They never again looked to the physical or the material things of the world.

Once they experienced the coming of God's Spirit into their beings, they never again asked about the earthly power. Experiencing the power of God within their lives was the utmost experience of their lives. Nothing else was ever needed.

Once God's Spirit truly takes up residence within a person, that person is fully satisfied. Nothing else can ever satisfy...not position...not recognition...not fame...nothing else!

When they were baptized with the Holy Spirit their focus changed to service and ministry. Instead of focusing upon themselves their focus was changed to the purpose God had given them to evangelize the world.

It is time for the Church to once again set our focus on fulfilling the purpose God has given us of proclaiming the Gospel of Jesus Christ in a demonstration of power to the nations of the world as an end-time witness.

It's time for the Church to get back to preaching the simple Gospel of Jesus Christ...crucified...risen...coming again.

The world doesn't need man-made doctrines... gimmicks...get rich schemes...or a watered-down, sugar-coated gospel.

The world desperately needs to hear and see a manifestation of God's power preached with signs and wonders accompanying it!

God Is Raising Up 'Ordinary' People To Be His Witnesses!

The prophecy God has given us is that before this decade closes, there will be a tremendous manifestation of the true Holy Spirit power of God. It will last for three years. A divine capability will once again be given to God's people...to show the world that Jesus Christ is the all-powerful Son of the living God, and that there is salvation, healing, and deliverance in His Name!

I believe God will raise up men and women, young people, and even children, who are so full of the power of God that they will reach thousands who are going to turn to God because of the mighty miracles that will be manifested through them. Because of their experience with God's destiny for their lives, they are becoming extraordinary people.

Just as God used the believers in the early Church to proclaim the Gospel to the nations of the world, I believe He is now raising up obscure, unknown individuals throughout the world...

- Who are hungry for God's power to be manifested through them...

- Who are 100 percent sold out to Christ...

- Who are willing to pay the price to help bring revival to their nations...

And He is empowering them...breathing a fresh anointing upon their lives so that they will be used as mighty end-time witnesses in the nations of the world.

One example of this is the testimony I received from my good friend, Dennis Balcombe, who is being used mightily in Asia. This testimony is of a young fourteen year old girl living in Inner Mongolia. This young girl accepted Christ and was eager to go out and preach the Gospel immediately. But, since she was so young, she was paired off with a 20-year-old woman.

These two travelled all over the countryside, preaching and witnessing to people.

One day they came upon a farm worker busy at work in the fields. They began to preach to this woman but she stopped them saying she had no time.

"Go inside the farm house and talk to the old woman lying in bed," she muttered irritably.

"Anna" was very excited! She had permission to preach!

She entered the house and shared the Gospel with the elderly woman, who kept nodding her head like she understood, tears streaming down her face.

Then the farm worker came rushing into the house, yelling at Anna, "She can't hear you, she's deaf!"

But Anna retorted, "No, she does hear me. Jesus can heal and He has healed her!"

The woman challenged her, "If indeed Jesus can heal people, then have Him heal her of paralysis. She has not left her bed for years.

Excited, Anna exclaimed, "Yes! Yes! Of course He can heal her!" She ran over to the old woman and grasped her hands, gently urging her to stand on her feet. The old woman stood, and slowly began to walk!

Because of this miracle the whole family accepted Christ and today, they have a house church in their home!

God Will Give You Power To Produce Proof!

The Holy Spirit was not given to the Church just so we can speak in tongues, rejoice, sing, dance, and have a good time in church.

Jesus did not send the Holy Spirit to the Church so we can simply enjoy the blessings of God in our lives. He intended for us to be baptized with the Holy Spirit so we will have power...

Power to be witnesses...

Power to produce the evidence that Jesus is Who He claims to be...

Power to fulfill the work of reaching a lost and dying world!

This is your end-time destiny.

You need not ever wonder or question concerning what God's purpose is for you in this end-time hour.

Whatever your experience has been in having God's power manifested through you, God wants to bring you into a new experience, where His power is flowing like a river out of your innermost being.

God has commissioned you to be an end-time witness. This is not a time to be sitting in a church pew soaking up the blessings of God. It is not a time to focus upon your needs and desires...your problems...your goals and plans.

God has called you to fulfill the great commission of evangelizing the world before Jesus comes. No. You do not have the power to fulfill this awesome responsibility. Forget your strengths and short comings. Forget your natural abilities.

You must have supernatural power.

God's unlimited, immeasurable power is needed. That is why Christ promised, "You shall receive power after the Holy Spirit is come upon you." Both the Spirit of God and His power are promised. The purpose of the Holy Spirit is to equip you to fulfill His purpose.

As a result of the power you receive through the Holy Spirit, you become a witness to the world as you proclaim the Gospel in a demonstration of power.

God has called every believer to be a witness wherever he is...in his home, church, community, and city. He has called every believer to give sacrificially so that the Gospel can be preached in the nations of the world and to use and support every means he can to reach the world.

Receive the promise of God's power manifested in your life, deep into your spirit. Position yourself to receive a fresh release of His power in your life in a greater dimension than you have ever experienced.

By faith, receive the dunamis power of God. Wait upon God and press through in the Spirit until you experience His power released within you.

Don't seek the power. Seek to be consumed by the Holy Spirit. Get rid of every hindrance and obstacle blocking you from drawing closer to Christ in an intimate relationship. His power will be released as the result of your relationship with Him.

Make a new dedication and commitment to God. Surrender yourself fully into His hands and step out in obedience to fulfill His will in this end-time hour.

Step into your end-time destiny!

In your home, on the job, at school, at the marketplace...wherever you go, be a witness of the power of God.

Every day of your life, ask God to open up new opportunities for you to share the Gospel, to pray for the sick, to speak the word of deliverance, and lead souls to Christ. Make winning souls and discipling them your greatest desire and top priority! Allow God's power to flow through you to meet the great needs within your community...city...nation!

CHAPTER SEVEN

God's Destiny For His Church...Divine Capability!

It is time for the true Church of Jesus Christ to come face to face with its destiny!

Jesus is coming very soon. And, before He comes, there will be an awesome manifestation of the destiny of God for His Church.

My question to the Church and to you is, "Are we ready?"

Are we ready as a Church to step into the destiny God has prepared for us?

When Jesus comes, He is not going to rapture a Church that is weak or anemic.

He will rapture a Church that has entered into the full purpose and the destiny God ordained for His Church before the earth was formed.

The Church will be raptured in the greatest demonstration...the greatest manifestation of the power of God the world has ever seen! It will supersede the demonstration and power in which the Church was born.

There will be an awesome demonstration and manifestation of the unlimited power of God. It will not last long. It will be a quick work. God will cut it short in righteousness.

The world will know that Jehovah is not the God of the past.

The world will know that Jesus is who He claims to be...the resurrected Son of the living God!

When the Church of Jesus Christ was born 2,000 years ago, God never intended it to know any limits!

The Church was born through an incredible, unique characteristic that gave it divine capability. God never intended to use our natural abilities. When He gave birth to this Church, He was giving birth to a Church that would have unlimited capability!

The reason why it would be unlimited is because it was divine! The power God released in the Early Church was not based on the natural man; it was based on divine capability.

When God gave birth to the Church, He never intended it to be like it is today.

God did not send His only Son, Jesus, to the earth to die on the cross and pay a 100 percent price so that the Church would be weak, anemic, powerless, and face one defeat after another.

Jesus Paid The Ultimate Price

Think about the ultimate price that Jesus paid to give birth to the Church. He purchased it with His own blood!

Can you see Christ in Gethsemane, travailing in agony until His sweat became great drops of blood falling to the ground?

As He agonized and poured Himself out before the Father, He was paying the price, surrendering His life so the Church could be cleansed and set free from every bondage of the enemy. He took upon Himself every sin, all the infirmities and weaknesses mankind would ever know, and carried them to the cross so that we would be totally cleansed...totally set free and never have to carry them any more.

Can you imagine what went through the heart of Father God as He looked down upon His Son, as the soldiers spit upon Christ, mocked Him and blasphemed His Holy Name?

Can you imagine the pain Father God must have felt as He watched the Roman soldiers take His only beloved Son, tie Him to a whipping post and beat Him unmercifully until the flesh was torn from His back and His blood spilled upon the ground?

Can you imagine the Father watching as the Roman soldiers beat Him with their fists and pull out His beard until His face no longer looked human?

Do you have any idea what went through His Father's heart as He watched His Son with the crown of thorns on His brow, struggling and falling under the heavy weight of the cross, as He carried it to Golgotha's hill?

Do you have any idea of the pain that pierced His heart as Father God heard Jesus' anguished cries, as the Roman soldiers nailed His hands and feet to the cross and thrust it into the ground?

Can you imagine what was in the heart of the Father as He watched Him hang on the cross in shame and disgrace, bearing the sins and disease of the world in His own body?

Father God paid a 100 percent price to give birth to a Church that would never experience one defeat! He paid the price for you so that you would no longer be vulnerable to the enemy or experience defeat.

Do you think for one moment that God paid a 100 percent price to give birth to an organization or a denomination run by man?

Do you think God paid a 100 percent price for His Church to live in 50 percent victory?

Jesus didn't pay a 25 percent price, a 50 percent price, or a 75 percent price. He paid a 100 percent price. He didn't pay that awesome price for what is preached in our churches today.

He didn't pay it for a 50 percent victory.

He didn't pay it for a 75 percent victory.

He paid it for you to experience 100 percent victory over 100 percent of the enemy 100 percent of the time!

As Christ hung on the cross, He was looking down the corridor of time to see the untold millions of sons and daughters who would be part of His glorious Church. "...for the joy that was set before him, endured the cross, despising the shame..." (Hebrews 12:2). He endured the agony and shame of the cross knowing that He was bringing "many sons into glory" (Hebrews 2:10) who would be transformed and conformed into His image (Romans 8:29).

God's Destiny For You...No Defeat!

When God gave birth to this Church, He did not give birth to an organization or denomination. He gave birth to an indestructible, supernatural superstructure that is a part of Himself.

He never intended that we would know any failure. You cannot show me one Scripture where the Early Church was defeated.

Persecuted...troubled...yes.

Tempted...tried...yes.

Beaten...imprisoned...yes.

Tortured...martyred...yes.

Defeated...never!

The believers in the Early Church faced every possible circumstance and attack of the enemy and were victorious. They faced suffering, hardship, imprisonment, torture and death. Yet they overcame through the power of the Holy Spirit working within them.

The Apostle Paul said,

> *We are troubled on every side, yet not distressed; we are perplexed, but not in despair; persecuted, but not forsaken; cast down, but not destroyed.*
>
> 2 Corinthians 4:8-9

In God's great plan for the Church, He did not allow His Son to pay the ultimate price to give birth to a Church that would be limited.

When God gave birth to the Church, He planned to raise up a people who were representative of His Son Jesus. Do you think for one moment, that if these people are to be representative of Jesus that God will allow them to be vulnerable to His enemy?

No! In His master design He planned to give birth to a Church that will have all power over all the power of his arch enemy, Lucifer! He never planned for Satan to defeat you one time!

God's Destiny For You...More Than A Conqueror

The Church of Jesus Christ was born in power. Don't ever forget that. It wasn't born anemic; it wasn't born spiritless; it wasn't born through education; it wasn't born through organization; it wasn't born through denominations. It was born through a demonstration of the power of the Spirit!

God has a destiny for you...that you will be not just a conqueror, but more than a conqueror through Christ who lives in you by His Spirit! Paul said, *"Yet amid all these things we are more than conquerors and gain a surpassing victory through Him Who loved us"* (Romans 8:37, AMP).

Does this Scripture reveal a 50 percent or 75 percent victory? No!

Christ paid a 100 percent price so that His Church will live in 100 percent victory.

We don't just have the victory. The word "conqueror" means not just to be a victor but to have more than just the victory. It means to go beyond the victory. God hasn't planned for you to just survive or get by.

There's nothing in the Word of God that shows us the character and nature of God is just to do the minimum. He has planned to do more than just give you the victory.

There is not one Scripture that reveals God has planned for us to experience defeat! In Jesus' Name, God has not planned one defeat for you! Not one!

The question is, "Are you ready to step into your destiny and take the 100 percent victory that is yours?"

Too many of God's people have been under severe attack. They have experienced attacks from the enemy, that have brought their spiritual life close to spiritual death, where they have been contemplating giving up.

The devil has a purpose in attacking your life. There are many Christians who are very close to a point where they have become so worn out, so weary, that they are ready to give up. They are not ready to give up their salvation, but are ready to give up on living that overcoming, powerful, fruitful life God planned for His Church.

Are you at this point in your experience?

Regardless of the circumstances, problems, trials, and heartaches you may be facing, God has destined you to be more than a conqueror! The Apostle Paul told the believers in Rome:

> *For those whom He foreknew [of whom He was aware and loved beforehand], He also destined from the beginning (foreordaining them) to be molded into the image of His Son (and share inwardly His likeness), that He might become the first-born among many brethren. And those whom He thus foreordained He also called; and those whom He called He also justified (acquitted, made righteous, putting them into right standing with Himself). And those whom He justified He also glorified [raising them to a heavenly dignity and condition [state of being]. What then shall we say to (all) this? If God be for us, who (can be) against us? [Who can be our foe, if God is on our side?]*
>
> Romans 8:29-31, AMP

Don't be a victim! God never planned for you to fail! Never! God planned for you to live in total victory.

I'm not talking about living a life that is totally free from the circumstances and the battles that we face. No!

Look at 2 Corinthians 4:8-9 AMP, Paul said:

> *We are hedged in (pressed) on every side [troubled and oppressed in every way]; but not cramped or crushed; we suffer embarrassments and are perplexed and unable to find a way out, but not driven to despair.*

"We are hedged in," Paul said, "on every side, troubled, oppressed in every way." But, we are not defeated!

The battle is raging, but you're not defeated!

The attack of the enemy is on, but you're not defeated!

It is how you react in the battle based upon what you know God has promised in His Word.

There's an anointing God has placed within us that is greater than all the power of the enemy. Christ is in you. And, because He's in you, that power is perfect, that power is pure; that power can never fail. Paul said,

> *...we possess this precious treasure (the divine Light of the Gospel) in (frail, human) vessels of earth, that the grandeur and exceeding greatness of the power may be shown to be of God and not from ourselves.*
>
> 2 Corinthians 4:7, AMP

We rejoice because the excellency of the power in us is not of man. It's not the jerk. It's not the jiggle. It's not the shout. The excellency of that power, the guarantee of that power, the exceeding greatness of that power is not because of us, it's because of Jesus, Who is in us!

An anointing of the Spirit of God is in you! Christ is in you! And greater is He that is in you, than he that is in the world!

Don't struggle, because you have already defeated the enemy!

You say, "But, how is it possible that I have already defeated him?"

You have defeated Satan and his principalities because of Christ Who is in you. Christ defeated him, so you defeated him!

There is no circumstance, no trial, no temptation, no persecution that Satan can ever bring into your life that can defeat you...when you have this relationship with Christ and know the victory belongs to you!

The price has been paid, but you must take hold of it and claim it for yourself through faith.

The God that you and I serve is able to do superabundantly above all that we can ever ask or think, according to His power working within us (Ephesians 3:20).

Why is it that we aren't seeing this truth fulfilled in the Church today?

What Happened To The Church?

The Church of Jesus Christ was born in a demonstration of divine capability that gave it power to turn cities upside down and evangelize the entire known world.

By the end of the third century, the Name of Christ was known, loved, and persecuted in every province and city of the Roman Empire. Constantine the Great, the ruler of the civilized world, laid his crown at the feet of Jesus.

Something happened in the third Century, and the flow of the miracle power of God began to diminish. We are going to look at some of the major reasons why God's power diminished within the Church, bringing it to a weakened position and also look at the condition of the Church today.

The congregation of Jerusalem became the mother church under the direction of the apostles, who were assisted by a number of presbyters, and seven deacons appointed to care for the poor and sick.

One of the major reasons for the Church's tremendous growth in the first three centuries was due to the fact that every believer accepted the responsibility to proclaim the Gospel to unbelievers.

There was no distinction made between the teachers and preachers and the other believers. Every believer could proclaim the Gospel and every Christian who had the gift could pray, teach, and exhort in the congregation.

The Holy Spirit moved within the entire congregation and was not confined to work only within a particular ministry office. Believers were daily in the Temple and in daily worship and fellowship from house to house.

And they, continuing daily with one accord in the temple, and breaking bread from house to house, did eat their meat with gladness and singleness of heart.

Acts 2:46

These believers were empowered by the Holy Spirit to fulfill the great commission. They possessed a holy zeal and commitment to fulfill the work of God.

Members within the Early Church considered themselves to be one family of God, and members of one body under one head, Jesus Christ. They were so united together in love, they sold all their possessions and goods and divided them according to every man's needs.

141

And all that believed were together and had all things common; and sold their possessions and goods, and parted them to all men, as every man had need.

Acts 2:44-45

It was the believers who were scattered and spread the Gospel to the other regions. The stoning of Stephen marked the beginning of the persecution against the Church. After his death, the believers were scattered throughout the regions, but the apostles remained in Jerusalem.

And they were all scattered aboad throughout the regions of Judea and Samaria, except the apostles... Therefore they that were scattered abroad went every where preaching the word.

Acts 8:1&4

Every where the believers went...in the marketplace ...house to house...the believers continued to proclaim the Gospel of Jesus Christ, with miracles as a living witness to the truth of the resurrection of Jesus Christ.

Until about the close of the second century the Christians held their worship meetings mostly in private houses, in desert places, at the graves of the martyrs, and in the crypts of the catacombs. By the middle of the third century, the number of believers had multiplied so rapidly it was necessary to build larger meeting places to accommodate the people.

The Church functioned as one body according to the direction and leading of the Holy Spirit. The major function of the fivefold ministry of the apostles, prophets, evangelists, pastors, and teachers was not to do the work of the ministry, but to disciple and build up the saints so they would be able to do the work of the ministry.

The Church wasn't centralized around the ministry of one or two leaders, it was a body ministry. The members of the Body were functioning together as one unit.

This was the way God intended the Church to function, with all parts of the Body mutually dependent upon one another, with Christ as the Head.

When Christ ascended into heaven, He placed the fivefold ministry within the Church for the purpose of bringing it to full maturity.

> *And he gave some, apostles; and some, prophets; and some, evangelists; and some, pastors and teachers; For the perfecting of the saints, for the work of the ministry, for the edifying of the body of Christ.*

> Ephesians 4:11-12

His purpose was that *"we all come in the unity of the faith, and of the knowledge of the Son of God, unto a perfect man, unto the measure of the stature of the fulness of Christ"* (Ephesians 4:13).

God never intended there to be a distinction of a special priesthood mediating between God and the laity. There is only one Great High Priest and Mediator between God and man...Jesus Christ. Every believer is considered part of a holy priesthood. Peter told the believers, *"But ye are a chosen generation, a royal priesthood, an holy nation..."* (1 Peter 2:9). John wrote that Christ has made us *"kings and priests unto God"* (Revelation 1:6).

The Apostolic Church functioned according to the direct revelation and leading of the Holy Spirit. There was a divine flow of the Holy Spirit energizing and mobilizing the apostles and disciples to fulfill the work God called them to do.

Multitudes were added to the Church as a result of the manifestation of the power of the Holy Spirit flowing through the apostles and believers to heal the sick, cast out devils, and raise the dead. They weren't relying upon their natural abilities and strength to direct the Church and fulfill the commission Christ gave them. There was a divine flow of the Holy Spirit, enabling them to boldly proclaim the Word and minister to the desperate needs of the people, while facing persecution and death.

A Man-Made Structure Was Substituted Instead Of God's!

In the second century, with the death of the apostles, major changes took place in the Church that weakened it. The old form of worship and tradition began to reassert itself. The Church started to organize and establish its own structure. Instead of relying solely upon Christ and looking to Him for His leadership, they began to follow man-made traditions and depend upon the arm of the flesh.

Within the new organization which was established, the emphasis upon the ministry of every believer began to shift with a new major emphasis focusing upon the bishop, priest, and deacon. The office of the bishop was elevated and the people were taught to unconditionally obey him and not do anything without his will. Disobedience to the bishop was considered apostasy from Christ, who was determined to act in and through the bishops. Without the bishop no one was to do anything connected with the Church. Salvation became pretty much dependent upon obedience to the bishop.

Three centuries later, Hilary of Arles, made salvation dependent upon obedience to the pope by declaring every person who rebelled against the pope to be a servant of the devil.

By the third century there was a clear distinction of a class of teachers apart from the believers. The term "priest" was used exclusively for ministers, especially the bishops. In

398 A.D., laymen were no longer allowed the freedom to preach or teach. They were prohibited from teaching in the presence of the clergymen and without their consent.

Instead of following the divine order and structure God planned for the Church, men instituted one based upon the natural mind.

Instead of allowing the Holy Spirit freedom to direct and build the Church according to God's divine purpose, men instituted rules and regulations giving them control.

As a result, the awesome manifestation of God's power that flowed through the Apostolic Church was quenched. Instead of the miracle power of God being manifested to heal the sick, cast out demons, and raise the dead, there were man-made forms and rituals.

Instead of every believer proclaiming the Gospel in a demonstration of power, the ministry of the Church was confined within the religious hierarchy established by men.

Instead of believers having a living, vibrant, personal relationship with God, based upon Christ's victory on the cross over sin, death, and hell, they were required to go through a priest as a mediator between them and God.

Instead of salvation based upon the blood of Jesus applied to their lives, people were taught salvation through good works and through the observance of the rituals and the sacraments of the Church.

When the Church started to organize and substitute man-made laws and traditions for the true move of God and His power and Presence, something happened in the spirit world. The anointing of the Church started to diminish.

Compromise And Paganism Polluted The Church

Perhaps the gravest danger the Church faced which greatly affected the flow of God's power was the secularization of the Church under the Emperor Constantine.

The Church faced nearly 300 years of the greatest and deadliest persecution in history in a war waged by Rome against Christianity. This persecution was a demonic-inspired war to stop the spread of Christianity and destroy the Church.

Under the emperors Trajan and Hadrian, circumcision was prohibited and Jerusalem was desecrated by the idolatries of the pagans. This provoked an uprising among the Jews. The rebel leader for the Jews was Bar-Cosiba, who caused the Christians who refused to join this rebellion to be murdered.

In 135 A.D., Emperor Hadrian's general defeated this Jewish rebel force and more than one-half million Jews were slaughtered. A great number were sold into slavery, nearly all Palestine laid waste, Jerusalem was destroyed, and a Roman colony was erected on the ruins with an image of Jupiter and a temple of Venus. Jews were forbidden to even visit the former Jerusalem upon penalty of death.

Beginning with Nero and ending with Diocletian in 313 A.D., multiplied thousands were tortured, beheaded, thrown to wild beasts, crucified, burned at the stake, and put to death by every cruel torture imaginable.

Under Decius' determined resolve to exterminate Christians, persecution was violent. Multitudes perished under cruel tortures in Rome, North Africa, Egypt, and Asia Minor.

The most severe persecution was under Diocletian. For ten years Christians were hunted in caves and forests. They were burned, thrown to wild beasts, and put to death by every cruelty possible to mankind.

The catacombs beneath the city of Rome, 8 to 10 feet wide and 4 to 6 feet high, were used for burial of Christians during the persecutions. There are estimated at between 2,000,000 and 7,000,000 Christian graves.

The persecution intended to annihilate the Church, God used instead to build it! By the end of the persecutions (313 A.D.) Christians numbered about one-half the population of the Roman Empire. Christians filled the Roman Empire. They were in its cities, towns, islands, tribes, palaces, and in their Roman assemblies and Senate.

The persecution ended and the entire Roman Empire surrendered to Christianity as the Emperor Constantine laid his crown at the foot of the cross.
In 313 A.D. he ordered the full restoration of confiscated church property at the expense of the Imperial treasury.

In his Edict of Toleration, Constantine granted to Christians, and all others, full liberty of following the religion of their choice. In 325 A.D. he issued a general exhortation to everyone in the Roman Empire to embrace Christianity and the whole Roman world became nominally Christian.

The Church united together with the very government that had tried to destroy it through 300 years of persecution. This was the beginning of the state-church system. The Church adapted its organization to the political and geographical divisions of the Roman Empire. The bishops became leading officers in the state and acquired a controlling influence in civil and political affairs.

In 376-395 A.D. Emperor Theodosius made Christianity the state religion of the Roman Empire and made Church membership compulsory. As a result, the Church was filled with unregenerate people with their pagan influences and practices.

The Church became polluted with Greek and Oriental heathen philosophies and many different sects arose: Gnosticism, Montanism, Arianism and many other "isms." The Church became paganized with the worship of images, relics, martyrs, Mary, and the Saints.

147

Ceremonialism, formalism, and man-made traditions were introduced; worship developed into imposing ceremonies similar to those belonging to heathen temples.

With the compromise and paganization of the Church, the power of God manifested in the Apostolic Church in the first three centuries, continued to diminish as it entered the Dark Ages.

During the Dark Ages, beginning in 1095 A.D., crusaders marching under the banner of Christianity, slaughtered thousands in their conquest of the Holy Land and the defeat of Islam.

In the first conquest, the streets of Jerusalem were filled with dead bodies. Jews were burned with their synagogues. The blood of the massacred in the Temple area reached to the knees and bridles of the horses.

These crusaders were designated by titles such as army "of the cross;" army "of Christ;" and crusaders were called the "soldiers of Christ."

This so-called army "of the cross" slaughtered with the sword, in the name of Christianity, everyone they found in Jerusalem and spared no one. The victors were covered with blood head to foot and it was estimated 40,000 to 100,000 were slain during the blood-bath.

The Church continued in its apostasy until the sixteenth century when God used Martin Luther to bring about the Reformation. Convinced that salvation and justification was by faith alone instead of by sacraments, good works, and mediation, on October 31, 1517 he posted 95 theses on the Church door at Wittenburg. This began an open attack on the doctrines and authority of the Catholic Church and a Reformation movement within the Church establishing Protestantism with it's emphasis on personal responsibility and placing people in direct communion with God.

Two distinct branches of Protestantism grew out of the Reformation: The evangelical churches of Scandinavia and Germany were followers of Martin Luther, and the reformed churches in other countries were followers of John Calvin and Huldreich Zwingli.

Throughout the centuries, with the establishment of Protestantism, differences have arisen in Church on doctrinal issues, and the various denominations which make up the Church today have developed.

God never intended the Church to be divided by doctrinal differences and denominationalism.

He never intended the power and anointing that was manifested in the Apostolic Church to diminish.

He never intended His miracle-working power, or the gifts of the Spirit, to cease functioning within the Church.

God intends there to be a continual flow of His unlimited, immeasurable power within His people today.

A New Demonstration Of The True Power Of Pentecost Is Coming!

Two thousand years ago, the Church was born with a unique characteristic that gave it a divine capability to produce the proof of the resurrection of Jesus Christ, the Son of the living God.

After the third century, the Church lost that experience. Today when we get the mask off and look at the condition of the Church, we cannot find a true demonstration of that same manifestation... the fire of Pentecost...the same demonstration of the Holy Spirit that gave birth to the Church.

It's missing!

Over the years, we have had a small taste of it. The outpouring on Azusa Street...glossolalia...the moving of the Holy Spirit breaking through denominational barriers with the Charismatic movement.

We have seen recent outpourings of God's Spirit...the Toronto blessing in Toronto, Canada...the Brownsville Revival in Florida, and have experienced awesome moves of the Holy Spirit in our meetings in the nations of the world.

However, what we have experienced is only a foretaste of what God has in store for His Church in this end-time hour. We haven't seen anything yet compared with what God is about to do!

We still have not seen the fullness of the true breakthrough of the power of Pentecost, the true baptism of the Holy Spirit.

But now something is about to happen! God is saying, "I'm going to do a new work among My people! There will be a new release...a new demonstration of my supernatural power!"

Since the third century, the Church has tried to contain the Holy Spirit within old wineskins...outmoded, man-made traditions...man-made philosophies.

The old wineskins of the Church structure have placed limitations upon the free-moving of the Holy Spirit. Instead of following the leading of the Holy Spirit, Christian leaders, pastors, evangelists, and ministers are bound by church politics. They are bound by tradition and their loyalty to their denominations.

Men have tried to confine the working of the Holy Spirit to their narrow concept and limited understanding of how the Holy Spirit should operate within the Church.

Over the years, the Church has "quenched" or tried to restrict the moving of the Holy Spirit because it does not fit within the framework of their doctrinal beliefs.

But, today is a new day for the Church!

The "old wineskins" of the Church structure, which have been binding and hindering the flow and demonstration of the power of God, is going to give way to the new!

God wants to do a new work in your life..to take you beyond your limitations...beyond your preconceived ideas...beyond your mental barriers and hang ups!

God never intended His power in your life to be limited. Believe me when I tell you, there is no limit to the power God desires to release within you.

NO LIMIT!

You are only limited to the degree you fail to accept God's promises and act on them.

God will do *"exceeding abundantly above all that we ask or think, according to the power that worketh in us"* (Ephesians 3:20). Paul said that God would far exceed ALL our expectations and our limited natural abilities to think or ask. How? According to His power working in us!

Paul was not talking about some remote force or power far removed from us somewhere in the heavens. He was referring to the dunamis miracle-working power of God Almighty residing within us by the Holy Spirit!

He was not referring to some latent, inactive power that fluctuates or changes from one day to the next, or that is dependent upon man's abilities. He was talking about the immeasurable, unlimited power of God that is an active force working within us to transform and empower us.

Through the indwelling of the Holy Spirit, the same mighty power that raised Christ from the dead is in you! God's power that is working for you and in you is according to the unlimited power God manifested in Christ when He raised Him from the dead. The resurrection power of Almighty God is in you!

Paul told the Romans, *"But ye are not in the flesh, but in the Spirit, if so be that the Spirit of God dwell in you..."* (Romans 8:9).

He said,

> *But if the Spirit of him that raised up Jesus from the dead dwell in you, he that raised up Christ from the*

dead shall also quicken your mortal bodies by his Spirit
that dwelleth in you.

Romans 8:11

God has planned for you to manifest His resurrection power to the world. He has given it to you and wants it to flow out of you. This is your spiritual destiny!

The great desire of the Apostle Paul's heart was, *"That I may know him, and the power of his resurrection..."* (Philippians 3:10). God wants you to know Him and the fullness of His resurrection power in you!

Paul said:

Now unto him that is able to do exceeding abundantly above all that we ask or think, according to the power that worketh in us.

Ephesians 3:20

God will do far beyond and above anything we can ever ask, or our minds can even conceive, according to His mighty resurrection power working in us!

The word, "power" in the above verse is translated from the Greek word, "dunamis." It refers to the supernatural power of Almighty God. It is the miraculous power, ability and might of God.

The same dunamis...supernatural, miracle working power of God:

- That was in Christ and manifested through
  Him in opening blind eyes, healing the sick,
  making the lame walk, and raising the dead
- That raised Christ from the dead
- That was poured out at Pentecost
- That was manifested in the lives of Peter,
  Paul and the other apostles and believers in
  the Early Church

...is the same power that is working within His Church today! It has not changed! It has not diminished in strength! It is the same! God's power hasn't changed, the Church has limited the flow of His power. We have tried to accomplish God's will according to our natural abilities instead of allowing His power to flow through us unhindered.

This dunamis miracle-working power of God is within. It is not something that is far removed, somewhere in the heavens, that is released upon us from time to time. It is within us.

God Has Destined You To Have The Same Power To Do The Same Works As Jesus!

God has shown me that a new manifestation of true Pentecostal power is coming upon the Church to restore us to the position of power and authority He planned us to have. The greatest outpouring of God's Spirit is yet to come!

In the next few years, there will be greater manifestations of the power and glory of God than we have ever experienced!

Thousands upon thousands will be saved, delivered, and healed on a gigantic scale!

God will work within the Church to bring us to a new level of maturity...a new level of spiritual authority and power...so that He can use us as a channel through which He can pour out His miracle-working power.

God has destined that the Church, you and I, His chosen people, be the means of bringing salvation, healing, and deliverance to the world.

Regardless of who you are...housewife, doctor, carpenter, secretary, business executive...

Regardless of how weak and insignificant you feel in your own strength...

Regardless of how young or old...God will do a new work in your life!

Do you really want to be used by God?

As Jesus was preparing to go to the cross, He told His disciples, *"...He that believeth on me, the works that I do shall he do also; and greater works than these shall he do; because I go unto my Father"* (John 14:12).

Jesus said we would do the same works and even GREATER WORKS!

Jesus was giving them a glimpse into the future. He was preparing them for the time when He would no longer be with them. He told them that because He was going to the Father, all those who believed on Him would be able to do the same works He had done and even greater.

Think about that for a moment! Jesus said that believers would have the same power, authority, and dominion to do the works He had done...

- To heal the sick
- To cast out devils
- To raise the dead
- To have authority over nature

Not only is Jesus now seated in heavenly places and has all power and dominion over all principalities; but as a child of God you have the same power and dominion! You are seated with Christ in heavenly places!

> *Even when we were dead in sins, hath quickened us together with Christ, (by grace ye are saved;) And hath raised us up together, and made us sit together in heavenly places in Christ Jesus:*
>
> Ephesians 2:5-6

This is the power God has given the true Church. God intends you to have the same unlimited power to do the same works that Jesus did, and even greater!

The Spirit of God is calling the Church today in this end-time hour, to take its position of power and authority to subdue and take dominion over all the power of the enemy!

For hundreds of years the Church has sat back with its hands folded while Satan has infested the earth with every form of sickness and sin imaginable...crime, rape, murder, abortion, sexual permissiveness, and drug and alcohol addiction.

Christians have been deceived into thinking that they are little insignificant "worms" who cannot do anything about the sin, sickness, and death that surrounds them. Few Christians understand their position of authority, and even fewer have been willing to step out in faith to exercise the power and authority God has given them.

But, today is a new day for the true Church of Jesus Christ! Are you ready to step into your end-time destiny?

How Far Do You Want To Go?

In 1996 when God showed me that this Decade of the Holy Spirit was about to close, He said to me, "Son, My people do not know My true Pentecostal experience."

When we get the mask off and look at the Church as it really is today, we see that we have a lot of joy, laughter, and other manifestations of the Spirit. These manifestations are wonderful. We need them. But, they are not evidence of the baptism of the Holy Spirit.

Ninety-nine point nine percent of the Christians sitting in our church pews have stopped at what I call, "the point of blessing."

For years the Church has had a limited understanding of the ministry, the work, the power, and the relationship of the Holy Spirit God intended for believers to experience. We have so much to learn about the ministry of the Holy Spirit, the blessed Third Person of the Trinity. Within the Pentecostal and Charismatic churches, the major emphasis has been focused upon the gift of tongues and the other manifestations of the Holy Spirit's power. However, too often we have not gone far enough to discover the depths and fullness of the relationship and inner working of the Holy Spirit... the Third Person of the Trinity.

We need to repent for the way we have treated the Holy Spirit. We have misunderstood Him, overlooked Him, quenched His power, and grieved Him.

Within the Body of Christ there has been a lack of understanding concerning the true Pentecostal experience and its purpose within the Church. This is one of the major reasons why we are not seeing more of God's miracle power manifested within our churches.

Something must happen to the Church of Jesus Christ!

We have form.

We have tradition.

We have "head knowledge." But the power is missing!

We must have a fresh outpouring of His Spirit that will give us an experience of power like the early Church experienced. Without this, we will not be able to reach the world!

The majority of Christians sitting in our church pews do not believe it is possible for God's miracle power to be released through them to heal the sick, open blind eyes, unstop deaf ears, or make the lame to walk.

Others have limited the experience of God's power to a manifestation of speaking in unknown tongues or some other outward manifestation.

Within the Church, we have placed limitations upon the working of God's Spirit in our midst according to how we think He should manifest His power. If there is an unusual move of the Spirit, or if we don't understand a particular manifestation of God's Spirit, we refuse to acknowledge or accept it.

Before we can experience the fullness of God's power working within us in the dimension He has purposed for us, we must have a fresh revelation of God's power working in us through the Holy Spirit.

"Head knowledge" is not enough! We can know all the Scriptures on God's power and the power we have in Christ by heart, quote them every day for the rest of our lives, and it won't get the job done.

"Head knowledge" of God's power will never heal the sick, open blind eyes, and break the bondages of drug and alcohol abuse!

It wasn't "head knowledge" that enabled Peter to say to the crippled man, lame from birth:

> Silver and gold have I none; but such as I have give I thee: In the name of Jesus Christ of Nazareth rise up and walk.
>
> Acts 3:6

No. It wasn't "head knowledge" that enabled that man to leap and walk. Peter had an experience of the dunamis power of God!

It's time for the Church to go beyond "head knowledge," to an experience where God's power and anointing is gushing forth out of our lives to heal the sick and break the bondage of sin in our cities.

We don't have time to play church!

We must press through in the Spirit until we have experienced a breakthrough of the power of God that will shake our world, as did the early Church.

Many Christians, once they have an experience where they speak in tongues, stop.

They say, "Praise the Lord; I've got it!" Instead of pressing on in the Spirit until the power of God is manifested in their lives, they sit back because they think they have "arrived," spiritually speaking, and glory in the manifestation of tongues. They are so filled with the joy of this experience that the real purpose of the Baptism of the Holy Spirit is overlooked. They stop at the point of blessing, when God has something far greater to possess them.

What Is The True Evidence Of Being Baptized With The Holy Spirit?

Contrary to what many believe, tongues...the prayer language of the Holy Spirit...is not the major sign that an individual has been "baptized" in the Holy Spirit. There are many Christians today who speak in unknown tongues on a regular basis, but who are still not operating in the power of God.

Did you know that it is possible for a person to be "filled" with the Holy Spirit...to have the "prayer language" of the Holy Spirit and to speak and pray in tongues regularly...and not be "baptized" with the Holy Spirit?

We must not, no never, minimize the beautiful manifestation of the gift of tongues or the "prayer language" of the Holy Spirit. Nor do I want to minimize the reason God gives us the ability to speak with other tongues. It is a dynamic gift of the Holy Spirit, given to the Church for a purpose:

> *For he that speaketh in an unknown tongue speaketh not unto men, but unto God...*
> I Corinthians 14:2

Praying in tongues...in the Spirit...builds us up in our faith (Jude 20). It enables us to have a direct communication with the Father when the Spirit prays for us.

Tongues is one of the gifts of the Spirit...word of wisdom, word of knowledge, faith, gifts of healing, working of miracles, prophecy, discerning of spirits, tongues, and interpretation of tongues (I Corinthians 12:8-10).

I praise God for the gift of speaking in tongues. I believe fully in the manifestation of the prayer language of the Holy Spirit. I pray in tongues every day of my life.

However, nowhere in the Scriptures will you find the promise of the Baptism of the Holy Spirit as given by Jesus Christ dependent upon the manifestation of the gift of tongues.

I am not trying to tell you that "other tongues" is not an evidence of what we call the infilling of the Holy Spirit. There is great scriptural evidence that this manifestation flowed through Christians in the early Church, as the Spirit manifested Himself in the life of the believer. What I am emphasizing is the fact that in the Church we have focused our attention on one of the manifestations of the Holy Spirit, rather than on the fullness and complete, unlimited, immeasurable work of the Holy Spirit Himself.

The evidence of being baptized with the Holy Spirit is power!

John the Baptist said:

> *I indeed baptize you with water unto repentance: but he that cometh after me is mightier than I, whose shoes I am not worthy to bear: he shall baptize you with the Holy Ghost, and with fire: whose fan is in his hand, and he will thoroughly purge his floor, and gather his wheat into the garner; but he will burn up the chaff with unquenchable fire.*
>
> Matthew 3:11-12

Being "baptized" and "filled" with the Holy Spirit are not the same. There are many Christians who have received an infilling of the Holy Spirit and have received the gift of the "prayer language" of the Holy Spirit, and some who have other gifts operating in their lives.

But there are very few Christians who have had an experience of power, where God's dunamis power is released within them to bring cripples out of wheelchairs...to open the eyes of the blind...to cause the deaf to hear and the dumb to speak.

One of the most effective ways that I have found to illustrate the difference between being "filled" and being "baptized" with the Holy Spirit is by using a glass of water and a pitcher full of water.

Look at the illustration of the glass of water on page 166. Imagine that this glass represents you. The water represents the Holy Spirit. It is possible for this glass to be filled full to overflowing but not be "baptized." The same is true in your life. It is possible for you to be filled full to overflowing with the Holy Spirit, but still not be "baptized."

Now look at the next illustration. What happens when you take the same full glass of water and place it in the pitcher full of water? It is BAPTIZED...IMMERSED... SUBMERGED!

This is what happens when you are BAPTIZED with the Holy Spirit...not only are you filled to overflowing with the Holy Spirit, but you are immersed...totally saturated with the Holy Spirit.

Are you hungry for God to baptize you with the Holy Spirit and power?

John the Baptist said concerning Christ;

> *I indeed baptize you with water unto repentance: but he that cometh after me is mightier than I, whose shoes I am not worthy to bear: he shall baptize you with the Holy Ghost, and with fire.*
>
> Matthew 3:11

John said, "I baptize you with water unto repentance, but there's somebody Who is coming after me Who had the promise of the Holy One. He is coming to tell you about the promise of God...that God said, "In the last days I will pour out of My Spirit on all flesh."

And what is He going to do? Is He going to give you a little bit? NO!

Is He going to give you a little bit more? Is He going to fill you with the Holy Ghost? No!

I tell you what He's going to do...He is going to baptize you!

Christ will baptize you with the Holy Spirit...Who will be with you and live in you! When He comes, something will happen in your life. No longer will you be the same...fearful...weak...defeated. You will have God's power flowing through you!

Do you know what the word "baptize" means? It means to be totally immersed...totally saturated. It means "to have the Spirit without measure." When you are baptized with the Holy Ghost and power, you can't measure it! You have it without limit!

WITHOUT LIMIT!

John said Jesus was coming to baptize with the Holy Ghost and with fire! He was talking about something more than just an emotional experience.

What Is This Baptism With Fire?

The baptism of fire is first of all a deep inner cleansing...a purging and burning out of the sin and ungodliness in our lives. This holy fire of the Holy Spirit is to burn continuously in our lives. Our lives...our wills...our thoughts...our motives...our innermost desires...are to be consumed by this fire until all that is left is pure, holy, and consecrated by God.

We must be consumed by the Holy Spirit before the power of God will be released in us.

On the Day of Pentecost, the fire of God fell upon the 120 disciples gathered together in the upper room, and they were baptized with the Holy Ghost and with fire! A holy fire began to burn within their innermost beings. Jesus told them, *"tarry ye in the city of Jerusalem, until ye be endued with power from on high"* (Luke 24:49).

As the fire of the Holy Spirit began to burn out the impurities...self, and the sin in their lives...they received power!

They were set on fire and received overcoming power to live a holy, consecrated life unto God!

They were set on fire and received Holy Ghost power to be His witnesses to the ends of the earth!

They were set on fire with a burning, all-consuming zeal to work the works of God!

They were set on fire with a holy love for Christ that could not be quenched, even though they were tested and tried through fiery afflictions!

On that day, as the tongues of fire rested upon them, their tongues were sanctified and set on fire to spread the Gospel to the world!

It is possible for you to be filled to overflowing but not be baptized with the Holy Spirit. When you are baptized you are totally immersed...totally saturated with the Holy Spirit.

It was the fire of the Holy Spirit burning within them that gave them holy boldness to preach the Word even after they were beaten and threatened by the high priest and the Sanhedrin. There was a fire within them which compelled them to speak...they could not be silenced!

It was the fire of the Holy Spirit burning in the life of Peter...cleansing...purging...purifying him, that released the power of God through him in such a powerful dimension, that as his shadow fell on the sick lying on cots, they were healed as he walked down the streets. The power of God flowed through him because he was a clean vessel, totally consumed by the Holy Spirit.

As the fire of the Holy Spirit burned within them, it burned out self until they were willing to lay down their lives for Christ and for one another. It was the fire of the Holy Spirit burning within Paul that enabled him to say of the manifold afflictions and the sufferings he endured for the sake of the Gospel, "None of these things move me, neither count I my life dear unto myself" (Acts 20:24). Paul's life...his will...his desires...his thoughts...his motives...were consumed by the Holy Spirit.

The fire of the Holy Spirit burning within them enabled the saints in the early Church to endure intense persecution and the fiery trials, afflictions and testings they experienced for the Gospel. They were tortured, crucified, beaten, imprisoned, thrown to the lions - yet they remained 100 percent consecrated and dedicated to God and His kingdom. They were not defeated! They were not moved by adversity, suffering, or pain. The fire of the Holy Spirit sustained and strengthened them and made them victorious even as they faced death.

Within the Body of Christ today, we must have this same Baptism of the Holy Ghost with fire to be able to fulfill the work God has given us to do and be prepared to face Christ at His coming.

Today we have the blessings...we have the shout...the dance...the tongues...the emotionalism...but the power is missing. God has not changed! The power of the Holy Spirit is the same today as it was on the day of Pentecost.

One of the major reasons the supernatural power of God is not being manifested in our lives as it was in the early Church is because we are seeking the power but not submitting to the purging flames of the Holy Spirit.

We want the power of God manifested in our lives, but we are unwilling to pay the price. Most Christians are eager for the blessings of God to be poured out in their lives, but they shrink back from the fire.

We must be willing to be stripped naked of everything that would hinder the work of God in our lives...that would hinder us from making a 100 percent dedication and consecration of all that we are and all that we have.

Self must die! Our desires...our plans...our wills...our jobs...our ministries...our families...our possessions...our lives...everything must be placed upon the altar of God.

Only then will the power of God be manifested through us.

Are you ready to step into your end time destiny?

Run To The Fire!

The fire that is coming to the Church will be a sovereign work of the Holy Spirit. As Christ's refining fire burns, it will separate the hypocritical, lukewarm Christians from the true believers. The Church will be sifted until there is an end-time remnant of people who are walking in holiness before God, who are wholly dedicated and consecrated to God.

This end-time remnant will go through a fiery baptism, where they will be tested and tried as gold is tried in the fire.

God spoke through Zechariah:

And I will bring the third part through the fire, and will refine them as silver is refined, and will try them as gold is tried: they shall call on my name, and I will hear them: I will say, It is my people: and they shall say, The Lord is my God.

Zechariah 13:9

Every true believer is going to go through the fire! Jesus said, "For every one shall be salted with fire, and every sacrifice shall be salted with salt" (Mark 9:49). Our faith will be tested and tried through the fiery trials we will face.

God is going to bring us through the fire... through fiery afflictions, trials, testings...not to punish, but to purify, strengthen, and perfect us. Those Christians who are not prepared for this baptism of fire, or who refuse to submit to the purging of the Holy Spirit will be shaken. Their faith will not stand the test.

This is not a popular message. It is not a message that will cause you to jump up and down or shout. But God is warning us by His Spirit so that we will be prepared. Regardless of what we may face, He has planned for us to be victorious.

Knowing this baptism of fire is coming, you must prepare yourself by submitting yourself to the Holy Spirit. Instead of shrinking back in fear from the fire, run to it! Cry out to God, as David did, *"Purge me with hyssop, and I shall be clean: wash me, and I shall be whiter than snow"* (Psalm 51:7).

Allow the Holy Spirit to strip away your pride...to expose the sin...weaknesses...any hypocrisy in your life. Ask God to reveal every area that has not been placed upon the altar of God...every impure motive...every fleshly desire that has not been crucified.

165

As the Holy Spirit exposes these things in your life, yield yourself to Him. Get rid of the sin. Ask Him to burn out every impure motive and attitude.

If you have become cold, lukewarm, or indifferent toward God, rekindle your love for Him. Don't withhold yourself from Him. Surrender yourself totally and renew your dedication and commitment to Him. Commit to Him every area of your life until self is crucified.

How hungry are you to experience a true manifestation of the Pentecostal power of God?

Do you want to be set on fire by the Holy Spirit, where God's power is manifested through you as it was through the disciples in the early Church?

Do you want to be set on fire until you have a burning compassion and zeal to win the lost?

Cry out to God right now...

"Consume me with Your holy fire! Burn out every sin...every impurity...everything that is displeasing to You. Consume my selfishness, my pride, my will. Set me on fire until I am consumed with a holy passion for You...until all that I am and all that I have are dedicated and consecrated to You. Fill me with a burning zeal and set my mouth on fire to spread the Gospel wherever I go. Consume me with Your holy fire until everything in my life is burned up and all that remains is pure and holy and acceptable to You."

Christ Is Coming To His Church With Fire!

If what we see in the Church today is all that God will do or all that He has planned to do in the Church, there is no hope for this world!

The time has come for the Church to face every weakness, every shortcoming, and every failure. We don't have to keep sweeping things under the carpet. It's time to strip ourselves of our pride and face the truth regarding our current condition. We don't fight it in our own strength, we can face whatever we need to face in the Name that is above every name, Jesus Christ, the Son of the living God!

The greatest danger the early Church faced was not the intense persecution. It was the compromise, idolatry, and sin that entered the Church that polluted it and brought it to a position of weakness. The greatest danger we face today is not persecution, it is the compromise, apathy, and sin that has weakened the Church.

Before Jesus comes for His Church, He is coming to His Church to restore divine order. I am not talking about His literal physical appearance at His second coming, but in a very unique and powerful manifestation of His Spirit within the Body of Christ before He returns.

Jesus is coming to the Church in this last hour with fire to purge, cleanse, and prepare us for His coming. Christ is coming in power and great glory to claim a bride that is pure, spotless, holy...without spot or wrinkle.

God cannot work His works through most of the believers in the Church today because of their condition. A clean engine is the only engine that delivers power.

I prophesy to you, we are the generation that will see two streams come together...the stream of the fire of Christ that comes back into the Church that will purge His people like a refiner's fire; and the stream of supernaturalism. After He has cleansed and purged us, He will flow through us in the greatest manifestation of His power the world has ever seen!

Christ sees the hypocrisy, covetousness, lukewarmness, apathy, and sin that is in the Church today.

He sees the compromise, indifference and self centeredness.

He sees the end-time seducing spirits that are in the Church.

The Church has become polluted by modern-day Pharisees and hypocrites who outwardly appear righteous...who talk the talk...but who are inwardly full of ungodliness, unclean thoughts and attitudes, and "hidden" sin.

Christ is going to expose it and burn it out of our lives until there is a pure stream of ministry flowing out of us.

A fire is coming to the Church...are you ready?

It is time for the Church to step into its end-time spiritual destiny...to go beyond the point of blessing into an experience of the true power of the Pentecostal experience.

Step into your end-time destiny!

CHAPTER EIGHT

Your Destiny...No Limits!

Church, the question we must answer is...

Why don't we see God's power flowing through us in the powerful dimension He has destined for us?

When we look at the experience of the Church today and compare it with what God has planned and all He has provided for us, we must ask ourselves what has happened to get us so far off course?

Nobody knows the pain of facing the reality of the issues of life today in our twentieth century more than we do.

When we look at the history of the Church and the things which brought it to such a weakened condition, we see that the greatest danger the early Christians faced was not the intense persecution lasting 300 years. It was during those years, in the first three centuries, the Church experienced their greatest growth.

It wasn't until the Church began to compromise with the world, organize, substitute man-made traditions, and depend upon their natural abilities instead of following the leading of the Holy Spirit, that the flow of the Spirit began to diminish.

My heart is so grieved...so burdened when I look at the true condition of the Church today. To think of the awesome price Jesus paid so that His Church would overcome every obstacle, every Satanic assault and fulfill His will upon the earth, and then to look at where we stand today!

Jesus defeated Satan...handed him over into our hands...

He has anointed us with the same Holy Spirit that was upon Him...

He equipped us with powerful spiritual weapons and sent us forth to make disciples of all nations.

But, after two thousand years, with all the tremendous technological breakthroughs...radio, television, satellites, computer technology...we still don't have the job done!

It's going to take a supernatural intervention of God on behalf of the Church to bring us from the position of weakness where we are today to the place of power He has planned.

I call upon all Church leaders, Pastors, Evangelists, Ministers, and Christians everywhere who are hungry to experience God's power flowing through the Church to the fullest extent in this end-time hour, to join me in repenting before God for the current condition of the Church.

It is time for the true Church of Jesus Christ to wake up, to rise up from where we are and take the position God has ordained for us.

Jesus is coming!

And, He is not coming for a lukewarm, wishy-washy, weak Church with an outward appearance of holiness and power, but that in reality, is impotent...powerless... unable to manifest the reality of the Gospel.

Only God knows the pathetic condition that exists in the Church today!

We are living in the midst of a modern-day Sodom and Gomorrah. Sin, corruption, perversion, sickness, and death surround us. Yet, the Church has fallen asleep. Our eyes have been diverted from our goal.

A spirit of compromise...

A spirit of complacency...

A spirit of worldliness...

A spirit of self promotion...

A spirit of indifference...

A spirit of covetousness...

...has entered the Church of Jesus Christ.

We must not be afraid to acknowledge our weaknesses and failures, repent of them and ask God to bring us to a new position of strength and power greater than we have ever known before!

It's time for us to stop playing church!

We don't have time to keep making excuses or to keep sweeping our weaknesses under the carpet!

This is our hour and we must step into our destiny!

The message God wants to break forth into your spirit is that when He gave birth to the Church 2000 years ago, He never planned for it to know any limits...not one!

When He gave birth to the Church, He never intended for members of the Body of Christ to depend upon their own limited abilities or natural resources.

When He breathed the Holy Spirit upon the 120 disciples gathered together in the upper room, He imparted a part of Himself, the Third Person of the Trinity, to live within them, giving them His unlimited, immeasurable power to fulfill His will upon the earth.

God has deposited within our spirits the same Spirit that was in Christ, which is a part of Himself! Jesus promised, *"I will not leave you comfortless: I will come to you"* (John 14:18). He said, *"At that day ye shall know that I am in my Father, and ye in me, and I in you"* (John 14:20).

> *Judas, not Iscariot, asked Him, Lord, how is it that You will reveal Yourself (make Yourself real) to us and not to the world? Jesus answered, If a person (really) loves Me, he will keep My word (obey My teaching); and My Father will love him, and We will come to him and make Our home (abode, special dwelling place) with him.*
>
> *John 14:22-23, AMP*

In essence, what Jesus was saying is that, "I'm coming to live in you. The world won't see Me, but you will know Me. You will know that I am living in you because the Holy

Spirit will reveal and manifest My very life in you. You're going to have a relationship with Me. I'm coming to you!"

Jesus told the disciples,

> *...And I will ask the Father, and He will give you another Comforter (Counselor, Helper, Intercessor, Advocate, Strengthener and Standby) that He may remain with you forever -The Spirit of Truth, Whom the world cannot receive (welcome, take to its heart), because it does not see Him, nor know and recognize Him. But you know and recognize Him, for He lives with you (constantly) and will be in you.*
>
> John 14:16-17, AMP

What this means to you and me is that God sent the blessed Holy Spirit...the Third Person of the Trinity to live and remain within us. The world doesn't recognize Him. They cannot perceive or know Him. But, we know Him because He lives continually in us and is working and manifesting Christ's life in us.

Jesus told His disciples, "When the Holy Spirit comes to live in you, He is going to be My Representative. He's going to speak the message the Father gives Him to speak. Not only will He reveal things that will happen in the future, He will reveal everything concerning Me and ALL that is mine!"

Look at John 16:13-15, in the Amplified Version Read it slowly and allow this revelation to break forth in your spirit:

> *But when He, the Spirit of Truth (the truth-giving Spirit) comes, He will guide you into all the truth (the whole, full truth). For He will not speak His own message (on His own authority); but He will tell whatever He hears (from the Father, He will give the message that has been given to Him) and He will announce and declare to you the things that are to come (that will happen in the future). He will honor and glorify Me, because He will take of (receive, draw upon) what is Mine and will reveal (declare, disclose, transmit) it to you. Everything that the*

Father has is Mine. That is what I meant when I said that He will take the things that are Mine and will reveal (declare, disclose, transmit) it to you.

Do you realize the significance of what this means to you?

There is no reason why you should ever be fearful, confused, or worried about the future.

There is no reason why you should ever be deceived or led astray by false doctrine.

There is no reason why you should ever question or doubt what God has planned for you.

There is no reason why you should ever be defeated regardless of the circumstances or problems you face.

There is no reason why you should ever again limit what God can and will do in you and through you!

When you have this experience where the Holy Spirit, Who proceeds forth from the Father, and is part of the Father, lives in you, and you enter into a relationship with Christ through Him, you have a supernatural, divine life flow within you that cannot ever be defeated!

Jesus said, "Everything that the Father has is Mine. The Holy Spirit is going to draw upon all that is mine and reveal it to you. You're going to have access to all that I have!"

When you are truly baptized with the Holy Spirit, there is an anointing that remains in you. It is holy...sacred. The Apostle John told the believers in the Church:

> *But as for you, the anointing (the sacred appointment, the unction) which you received from Him, abides (permanently) in you... But just as His anointing teaches you concerning everything and is true and is no falsehood, so you must abide in (live in, never depart from) Him (being rooted in Him, knit to Him) just as (His anointing) has taught you (to do).*

> I John 2:27, AMP

173

That sacred anointing is the Holy Spirit God has given to His Church, the same anointing that was upon Jesus. God anointed Him with the Holy Ghost and with power (Acts 10:38).

There are no limits...the power of the Holy Spirit in you is unlimited!

How far do you want to go?

God Knew We Would Need A Supernatural Power!

God sent Jesus to this earth for a divine purpose. In accordance with God's plan before the foundation of the earth, Jesus came to destroy the works of the devil, redeem men from sin, and restore us into full fellowship with the Father as His children.

> ...*For this purpose the Son of God was manifested, that he might destroy the works of the devil.*
>
> I John 3:8

Jesus didn't come to earth to inflict a wound on Satan or to bruise him. Jesus came here to defeat and destroy him.

Jesus said, "My meat, my purpose, the reason I am coming to this earth is to do the will of Him that sent me."

He told the Pharisees, "*...I proceeded forth and came from God; neither came I of myself, but He sent me*" (John 8:42).

He said, "*...I am not come of myself but he that sent me is true, whom ye know not. But I know him, for I am from him and he hath sent me*" (John 7:28-29).

God sent Jesus with a divine commission. But, He did not come with all His heavenly attributes. Although He was God in the flesh, He came to earth in the form of flesh and blood. He stripped Himself of His divine attributes and came as a man.

> *Who, although being essentially one with God and in the form of God, (possessing the fullness of the attributes which make God God), did not think this equality with God was a thing to be eagerly grasped or retained. But stripped Himself (of all privileges and rightful dignity) so as to assume the guise of a servant (slave), in that He became like men and was born a human being.*

> Philippians 2:6-7, AMP

Jesus, the living Word, Who was with God from the beginning, became flesh.

> *In the beginning was the Word, and the Word was with God, and the Word was God. The same was in the beginning with God. All things were made by him; and without him was not any thing made that was made. And the Word was made flesh, and dwelt among us.*

> John 1:1-3, 14 KJV

Jesus was God in the flesh, yet He did not rely or draw upon His divine abilities to destroy the works of Satan. When He healed the sick, raised the dead, and cast out devils, He did not use His divine abilities as the Son of God.

There is no record of Christ performing one miracle until He was first anointed with the Holy Ghost and power.

God knew His Son Jesus needed a supernatural power.

Jesus was the first to partake of the power of the blessed Third Person of the Trinity. He was filled and then equipped.

When He was baptized in the Holy Spirit in the River Jordan, the Holy Spirit came from heaven to live within Him. He rose up out of the water. The heavens opened, the Spirit of God came forth from the Father (Luke 3:21-22).

God came upon Him in the beautiful form of a dove. He had no sin in Him; He had not sinned. Jesus stood there gazing up into heaven and saw the Spirit descending in the form of a dove. He heard the voice of His Father as it resounded throughout the heavens, "Thou art my beloved Son, in whom I am well pleased."

Jesus was saturated. He was full of the Holy Ghost! From that day, Jesus was fully yielded and fully controlled by the Spirit.

> *Then Jesus, full of and controlled by the Holy Spirit, returned from the Jordan, and was led in (by) the (Holy) Spirit For (during) forty days in the wilderness (desert), where He was tempted (tried, tested exceedingly) by the devil. And He ate nothing during those days, and when they were completed, He was hungry.*
>
> Luke 4:1-2, AMP

From that day He walked continuously under this anointing.

When He walked out of the River Jordan, He was fully equipped. He was ready!

"Ready to do what, Brother Cerullo?"

He was ready for the task!

"What was the task?"

To witness of the Father to the world. To fulfill the purpose for which the Father sent Him. He was ready to destroy the power of the enemy! He was ready!

Jesus Was Fully Equipped To Destroy Satan's Power!

Before God sent Jesus forth to destroy the works of Satan, He anointed Him with the Holy Spirit. Do you think for one minute that God would send Jesus, His only begotten Son, to face the enemy without first equipping and giving Him the necessary weapons to destroy Satan?

The first thing Jesus did in Luke, chapter 4, is this: He was led by the Holy Spirit for forty days into a wilderness. There, He was tempted...tested...tried. Satan came against Him. He buffeted Him. But Jesus met every test and every trial. He faced and defeated Satan under the powerful Presence, manifestation, and anointing of the Holy Spirit which was in Him, until Satan had to flee.

When He came out of that experience, He didn't come out like most Christians do when they think they have an encounter with the enemy. He didn't come out like a wet dish rag. He didn't come out and say, "Whew...I tell you, that was a terrible battle I just had. I need to take a three month sabbatical."

When the enemy fled, Jesus went back to Jordan and started for his home town to continue His ministry with this power. Nothing leaked out. He came out of that experience full of the Holy Ghost!

> *And Jesus returned in the power of the Spirit into Galilee: and there went out a fame of him through all the region round about.*
>
> Luke 4:14

Jesus went from the experience of being baptized ready to meet the devil. He met him. He defeated him. He destroyed him! Then, when He came out of that experience of fasting forty days, He wasn't weak, falling all over Himself. He was full of the Holy Ghost, ready to go!

It was this Anointing, the indwelling Spirit of the living God abiding within Jesus, that was released from within Him which healed the sick.

It was that abiding Spirit of the Holy Ghost which was inside Him that cast out the devils.

He was not confused and He was not in doubt regarding the power. When the true manifestation of the

Holy Spirit abides in you and you are really experiencing the power, you will never ever doubt the power.

You will not be confused about the power. And you will not be confused about your prayers, either. You won't wonder about God's will. You won't wonder about healing the sick. The Holy Spirit living within you will pray through you the perfect will of God! (Romans 8:26-27)

Jesus was not intimidated. He didn't care one iota what the religious leaders thought of Him. He didn't care. He wasn't disturbed. He wasn't intimidated. He didn't try to be defensive. He didn't try to prove anything. He wasn't afraid to publicly say "I'm anointed. I'm sent from God. I've come here to destroy the power of the devil!"

As soon as He came out of the wilderness, He confronted the devil, and as soon as He got back to his home town He ran into the synagogue and opened the book and boldly proclaimed Who He was and His purpose.

Why?

Because He had just come from the Jordan. The heavens had opened. Something was inside Him. The Holy Spirit took His residence inside Him. He went out into the wilderness and found out that it worked. He was ready to open the Scroll in the synagogue and read the prophecy concerning Himself.

Publicly, in the synagogue, Jesus read:

> *The Spirit of the Lord is upon me, because he hath anointed me to preach the gospel to the poor; he hath sent me to heal the brokenhearted, to preach deliverance to the captives, and recovering of sight to the blind, to set at liberty them that are bruised.*
>
> Luke 4:18-19

Jesus said, "He hath sent me...this day. Not tomorrow...this day! You're going to know that I know Who I am. You're going to know that I know the purpose for which I am here. You're going to know that I know all power is given unto Me. You're going to know this day is this Scripture fulfilled. Not tomorrow. It's not for somebody else. I am the Christ."

From the moment Jesus was anointed, He was able to start fulfilling the purpose that God sent Him to this earth.

Church, until we experience this same baptism of the Holy Spirit, the true power of Pentecost, we will never be able to fulfill the purpose Christ has given us.

God Placed The Same Unlimited Power In His Church!

God knew when His Son came to earth He would have to face the task of doing His will, face the task of defeating the devil, and face the task of representing the Father here on this earth. God knew His Son would need supernatural power! That is why He anointed Him with the Holy Ghost and power.

God also knew His Church would need a supernatural power to fulfill His purposes and be a full manifestation of Christ to the world. And, He has planned for us to have the same power and anointing. There is no possible way we will be able to fulfill the purpose God has for us without this same supernatural manifestation in our lives.

God has planned for the same unlimited power that was in Christ and manifested through Him in opening blind eyes, healing the sick, making the lame walk, and raising the dead...

The same unlimited power that raised Christ from the dead...

The same unlimited power that was poured out at Pentecost...

The same unlimited power that was manifested in the lives of Peter, Paul, and the other apostles and believers in the early Church...

To be manifested within the end-time Church.

This is God's destiny for us today!

This is the destiny God has for you.

This is what God planned for His church before the earth was formed. Now, in this end-time hour He is going to raise up a remnant from the weakened, compromising Church today and will bring us to a position of full maturity where we will be a full manifestation of Christ to the world!

How far do you want to go?

Why Have We Allowed Compromise To Weaken Us?

God has implanted His Spirit within us giving us His unlimited, immeasurable power to fulfill His end-time plan!

Christ has given us His power and authority to do the same works He did and greater!

He has planned for the Church to be invincible...the most powerful force upon the earth!

Christ has destroyed the works of the devil and He has planned for us to manifest His power in ministering to the desperate needs of the world...healing the sick...casting out devils...proclaiming the Gospel in the nations in a demonstration of His unlimited power.

God gave birth to a Church that would know no limits!

Why have we allowed compromise into the Church?

Why have we compromised concerning divine healing?

Why have we limited and denied the Almighty power of God to heal?

There is probably no other doctrine that has been so attacked...both from within the Church and from without.

The Church denies the power to heal and the world ridicules those who lay hands on the sick.

There are many Christians who do not believe divine healing is for today. They believe the gift of healing was only manifested within the early Church. Then, there are those who preach it, but do not see the results manifested.

The God you and I serve is a God Who knows no limit!

He is a healing God!

He is the same yesterday, today, and forever!

There is not one Scripture that reveals God ever planned for His healing power to ever stop flowing through His Church.

Jesus paid a 100 percent price so that the Church would have 100 percent victory over 100 percent of the enemy 100 percent of the time!

He didn't leave us vulnerable to the attacks of the enemy. He anointed us. He equipped us. He empowered us with the power over all the power of the enemy! (Luke 10:19)

When God created man, there were three things God never intended him to possess: sin, sickness, and death. Man was created in the image of God, without sin. There was no pain, sickness, or death. God never intended man to know sickness. He never planned for man to have cancer, diabetes, arthritis, lung disease, heart disease, or any of the other sicknesses that are afflicting a vast majority of Christians in the Church today.

God didn't plan for His Church to be sick!

Sin, sickness, and death came as the result of man's fall in the Garden of Eden.

But, God sent Jesus to earth with a divine purpose.

...For this purpose the Son of God was manifested, that He might destroy the works of the devil.

1 John 3:8

181

Jesus faced Satan and destroyed him! He broke the power of sin, sickness, and death. He fulfilled His purpose. He took the stripes on His back. He took upon Himself all our sicknesses and diseases and carried them to the cross.

He was wounded for our transgressions, he was bruised for our iniquities: the chastisement of our peace was upon him; and with his stripes we are healed.

Isaiah 53:5

With His stripes we are healed!

The Power Of Sickness Has Been Broken!

The time has come for God's people to practice what they preach! It is one thing to preach divine healing and to say we believe God heals today, but an altogether different matter to go beyond head knowledge to see God's power released and healing manifested.

Jesus manifested God's healing power to the world. He went throughout Galilee and Syria healing all manner of sickness and disease. His fame spread throughout the land that He had power to heal and multitudes of people followed Him to hear His teaching and be healed.

He opened blind eyes, unstopped deaf ears, and caused the lame to walk.

He cast out demons and raised the dead.

There was no devil, no sickness, or disease that could withstand His power.

Everyone who came to Him was healed!

He fulfilled the word spoken through the Prophet Isaiah concerning Him that He would remove our sickness and disease.

...they brought unto him many that were possessed with devils: and he cast out the spirits with his word,

and healed all that were sick: That it might be fulfilled which was spoken by Esaias the prophet, saying, Himself took our infirmities, and bore our sicknesses.

Matthew 8:16-17

God's destiny for His Church is that we will be a full manifestation of Christ to the world. He plans for us to be His witnesses...to produce proof, through the manifestation of His power flowing through us, of His power to save, deliver, and heal all manner of sickness and disease.

How can we be a full representation of Christ to the world if we fail to proclaim divine healing in His Name, and have His power flowing through us to heal the sick and cast out devils?

Christ gave the Church the same power and authority He had to heal the sick in His Name. Before He ascended into heaven He said, *"...all power is given unto me in heaven and in earth"* (Matthew 28:18).

He commissioned His disciples to preach the Gospel to every creature and then He told them that signs would follow the believers. Jesus intended for His power to flow through every believer, not just evangelists, pastors, and the five-fold ministry. He said, believers will cast out devils in His Name, speak with new tongues and *"they shall lay hands on the sick, and they shall recover"* (Mark 16:17-18).

Are you ready to step into your destiny?

The healing power of God was manifested in the early Church. One of the first acts recorded after the Day of Pentecost was Peter healing the beggar who had been lame from his birth, forty years.

Everywhere they went, the people proclaimed the Gospel with signs following. Multitudes came to Jerusalem from surrounding cities bringing the sick and demon oppressed. They laid the sick on beds and couches in the streets to be healed. *"...And they were healed every one"* (Acts

5:16). The unlimited power of God was flowing through the Church to heal all who were sick and oppressed by the devil.

There was such a flow of God's power through Peter that when his shadow fell on the sick they were healed (Acts 5:15).

God manifested His healing power through Paul in such a powerful dimension that they took handkerchiefs and cloths which had been placed on his body, placed them on the sick and demons were cast out and people were healed (Acts 19:11-12). One of the major reasons for the tremendous growth in the Apostolic Church during the first three centuries was because of the miracles of healing which accompanied the preaching of the Word. The people believed the message of the Gospel because God bore witness through the miracles of healing in Jesus' Name!

The world is waiting for someone today with a true manifestation of God's power!

No More Excuses...No More Compromise!

God never intended for His healing power to be limited or to cease flowing in the Church. In this end time hour as He brings the Church to full maturity, He will release His healing power through members of the Body of Christ. There will be a wave of healing power that will encompass the world resulting in a great harvest of souls.

The time has come where the Church must stand and declare "thus saith the Lord!" No more compromising the Word! Either we believe divine healing is provided for all in the atonement or we don't. We must stop denying the power of God, stop making excuses for our failures, and have an experience where we are baptized with the same power that was flowing through the early Church!

When God raised up Israel He established a covenant with them based upon His Word. That covenant left no place for the enemy. It left no place for defeat. It was a covenant based on Jehovah God! He revealed Himself to His people as Jehovah Rapha. He said, *"...for I am the Lord that healeth thee"* (Exodus 15:26).

He told them, Obey Me. Keep My Law and not one disease that exists in this world will touch you. God promised to remove sickness form their midst. *"And the Lord will take away from thee all sickness..."* (Deuteronomy 7:15)

In the wilderness God provided healing for the children of Israel. When the brazen serpent was lifted up as a provision for their disobedience that brought sickness, every one that looked upon the brazen serpent was healed. (Numbers 21:8-9)

God did not give birth to the Church on any less of a Covenant than He did with the House of Israel. He gave us a better Covenant established on better promises because they were sealed with the blood of Jesus.

Healing belongs to the Church. Jesus paid the price! He destroyed the works of the devil! In His Name every sickness and disease must bow!

God never intended His children to have cancer!

He never intended for us to have ulcers!

He never intended for us to suffer with high blood pressure or hardening of the arteries!

He never intended for our bodies to be afflicted with sickness or disease!

When He gave birth to His Church, He gave birth to a Church with a price that was paid in full by Jesus Christ, the Son of the living God!

Jesus came here for a purpose! He didn't wound the devil. He destroyed him! You have a Covenant with Christ, your healer!

Sickness has no power over you!

Death has no power over you!

Jesus destroyed the power of the devil!

When you understand the Covenant of healing you have with God through Christ, you will walk in a new dimension in your spiritual life. When the enemy tries to put sickness or disease upon you, you will reject it. And, you won't be running to the doctors to get rid of it.

Your Covenant isn't with the Medical Association. If the enemy tries to put sickness upon you, don't run to the medicine cabinet, run to Jesus! Your Covenant is with Jesus! Your covenant is based upon the Word that says "by His stripes you are healed!"

It's Time To Stomp On The Devil!

It's time for the Church of Jesus Christ to take a stand and boldly declare to the world that there is healing in Jesus' Name! Instead of becoming intimidated and backing up when the world doesn't understand and starts criticizing and ridiculing us for praying for the sick and casting out devils, we must fearlessly proclaim the truth.

Ninety percent of the Church today retreats and is afraid of the criticism and ridicule. When the news media criticizes us, the Church gets confused and starts to accuse each other. They begin to point their finger and criticize. "If that brother was in the will of God, He wouldn't be persecuted. If that brother was in God's will, the newspapers wouldn't be tearing him apart."

How are we in the Church today going to stand against the powers of unbelief?

How are we going to stand against the ungodly forces that are permeating our society?

We aren't going to stop homosexuality by getting on a soap box or marching down a street carrying a sign.

We aren't going to stop abortion, alcohol and drug abuse, or pornography by having marches, signing petitions, or picketing outside abortion clinics, whorehouses, or x-rated movie theaters.

We aren't going to win the battle using carnal weapons. We aren't going to win using our natural abilities. We are going to use the mighty weapons of warfare God has given us that are mighty through God to the pulling down of strongholds.

We are going to win the battle through the unlimited power of God flowing through us! God never intended to use our natural abilities. It's time for us to move from the natural into the supernatural!

It's time for the Church to take a stand. No more compromise! No more intimidation! We're growing up to full maturity.

Instead of backing down, we need to let the enemy know we are a militant Church. We are an army of God! It's time for us to start stomping on the devil!

The weapons God has given us are not the weapons of this world. They have divine power to demolish strongholds and destroy arguments.

> *For though we walk (live) in the flesh, we are not carrying on our warfare according to the flesh and using mere human weapons. For the weapons of our warfare are not physical (weapons of flesh and blood), but they are mighty before God for the overthrow and destruction of strongholds, (inasmuch as we) refute arguments and theories and reasonings and every proud and lofty thing that sets itself up against the (true) knowledge of God; and we lead every thought and purpose away captive into the obedience of Christ, (the Messiah, the Anointed One).*
>
> 2 Corinthians 10:3-5, AMP

We don't argue.

We proclaim the unadulterated, uncompromising Word of God!

We must not be afraid to preach against the sins of lust, homosexuality, hatred, covetousness, and other sins that have infiltrated every area of our society and call for repentance.

We must not be afraid to proclaim to the humanistic, idolatrous society we live in that there is only one God...not Buddha...not Shinto...not Mohammed...He is God Jehovah, the God of Abraham, Isaac, and Jacob. And, there is only one way to salvation...Jesus Christ, the Son of the living God!

We must not be afraid to preach divine healing, deliverance, and the baptism of the Holy Spirit with the manifestation of His unlimited power.

We must cast down everything that exalts itself above the knowledge of God and take captive every thought and make it obedient to Jesus!

We must continue to heal the sick!

We must continue to cast out devils!

We must continue to tear down the enemy strongholds over our neighborhoods, cities, and nations in Jesus' Name!

Are you ready?

This is our time! We are going to rise up to our spiritual destiny and be the powerful force in this world God intended us to be!

CHAPTER NINE

A Fire Is Coming...Are You Ready?

Before we can step into the end-time destiny God has for us, we must be willing to take an honest look at the true condition of the Church and get rid of the compromise that has gained a stronghold.

We must have a new vision of Christ as He is today. When John saw Christ in a vision, he fell on his face before Him as if he were dead. He described Christ as having hair white as snow and eyes as a blazing fire, *"...and out of His mouth went a sharp two-edged sword"* (Revelation 1:16).

Do not be deceived. Christ, with His blazing eyes of fire, is walking in the midst of His Church today. Nothing is hidden from His penetrating gaze, as it pierces through the exterior of our lives into the innermost depths of our spirits.

Jesus told the Church in Pergamos, *"I know thy works and where thou dwellest..."* (Revelation 2:13).

He knows our works. He sees the hypocrisy, covetousness, lukewarmness, and sin that are prevalent in the Church today, and He is going to expose it and burn it out of our lives.

He sees into the deep, innermost recesses of our beings. He knows our thoughts, our motives, and our desires. It is foolish to try to hide or make excuses for the sin in our lives. NOTHING is hidden from God.

Nothing in all creation is hidden from God's sight. Everything is uncovered and laid bare before the eyes of him to whom we must give account.

Hebrews 4:13, NIV

Before Christ returns, He is coming with fire to purge, cleanse and prepare the Church so that we will not be consumed with fires of judgment. Do not be deceived. Christ is coming in power and great glory to claim a bride that is pure, spotless, holy...without spot or wrinkle.

Paul told the Ephesians:

> *...as Christ also loved the church, and gave himself for it; That he might sanctify and cleanse it with the washing of water by the word, that he might present it to himself a glorious church, not having spot, or wrinkle, or any such thing; but that it should be holy and without blemish.*
>
> Ephesians 5:25-27

God showed me that one of the Five Waves of the Spirit that are coming to the Church in this decade of destiny is a new wave of true holiness!

A spirit of true holiness, righteousness, and consecration on a new level is coming to the Body of Christ to prepare us for Christ's coming. There will be no more compromise or hypocrisy. Emotionalism will be replaced by serious dedication.

Jesus is not coming to receive a harlot bride that is committing spiritual adultery. He is not coming for a bride that has become polluted with the sinful lusts and desires of this world. He is coming for a holy end-time remnant...a people who have been cleansed and purified...without spot or blemish.

Christ intended for the Church to set the moral standards for the world. He said,

> *Ye are the salt of the earth: but if the salt have lost his savour, wherewith shall it be salted? it is thenceforth good for nothing, but to be cast out, and to be trodden under foot of men.*
>
> Matthew 5:13

190

Instead of the Church setting the moral standards, we have allowed Hollywood to do it!

Many Christians have compromised by allowing ungodly, immoral programs and R-rated movies into their homes. They "feed" on a steady diet of vulgar language, violence, illicit sex, and soap operas.

As a result:

There is a spirit of adultery...

There is a spirit of fornication...

There is a spirit of uncleanliness and ungodliness in the Church!

Instead of the Church taking a stand against the immoral, ungodly standards of the world, it is embracing them. Things which the Church once considered disgraceful or immoral, such as fornication and adultery, we tolerate in the Church instead of exposing and dealing with it according to the Word.

The Church, which once took a strong stand against divorce, has almost the same rate of divorce as the world, and it may be even higher.

There is a laxity concerning the sanctity of marriage with Christians becoming involved in extra-marital affairs...pastors leaving their wives and running off with other men's wives and condoning their actions! This immorality has spread into our government and armed services. But, how can we take a stand and set the standard when we allow the same sins to go unheeded and undisciplined?

The Church, as a whole, has not taken a strong united stand against the innocent killing of unborn babies through abortion. In fact, many of the young teenage pregnancies involve girls who have been raised up in church. Many churches, instead of teaching high moral standards and abstinence of sex before marriage, have relaxed and compromised with the world's standards.

Christ Is Coming To His Church With Fire!

The Church is filled with hypocrisy, lukewarmness, indifference, and self-centeredness. We are spending more time on ourselves, our homes, our automobiles, educating our children, taking care of what the devil has masterminded us to believe is our first priority.

We have covered our spirits with delusion and deception, and I tell you, Jesus is coming to His Church with a fire! That fire has already started. It is already taking place in the so-called leadership. God is purging the leaders. He is purging the shepherds who go under the guise of that name, but do not have shepherds' hearts.

Judgment is going to begin within the Church. Peter wrote,

> *For the time is come that judgment must begin at the house of God: and if it first begin at us, what shall the end be of them that obey not the gospel of God?*

> I Peter 4:17

Christ has started within the leadership because He cannot stand the hypocrisy. The sheep are suffering because the shepherds...the leaders... are sitting in high places. They have removed themselves from the people and many are more concerned about their own welfare...more concerned about building their own "kingdoms"...than they are about the spiritual welfare of the people in their congregations.

The sheep are starving...wounded...scattered... and have fallen prey to the enemy, while so-called shepherds have sat at ease. The sheep have wandered away and the shepherds have failed to seek them out to strengthen them. For fear of losing their position, they have failed to warn the sheep of danger and many have fallen by the wayside.

Christ came to bring fire upon the earth. God sent Him with the purpose of refining and purifying His people. God spoke through Malachi,

...For he is like a refiner's fire, and like fullers' soap: And he shall sit as a refiner and purifier of silver: and he shall purify the sons of Levi, and purge them as gold and silver...

Malachi 3:2

Malachi prophesied that Christ would come as a refiner's fire to purge and purify His people. John said:

...he shall baptize you with the Holy Ghost, and with fire: Whose fan is in is hand, and he will thoroughly purge his floor, and gather his wheat into the garner; but he will burn up the chaff with unquenchable fire.

Matthew 3:11-12

Whose floor is Christ going to purge? His floor!

Whose wheat is He going to gather? His wheat!

This is not a message concerning the wicked or unbelievers, the chaff are the hypocrites among the true believers...the professing, lukewarm Christians. The fire that is coming will purge or cleanse true believers and will separate the chaff...the hypocrites from the true believers and bring judgment and the fire of God's wrath upon them.

There is a fire coming! Are you ready for it?

Jesus has kindled that fire and today it is burning.

We Do Not Have Time To Play Church!

Religious systems are coming under this fire. Paul recorded in Acts the results of the fire of God which burned through a religious system in its day, and this fire is coming to burn through the religious system in our day! The structure of the Church is going to change.

Jesus said, "I am come to send fire!"(Luke 12:49).

The purpose of this fire that is coming to His Church is:

1. To purify and cleanse.
2. To reveal sin and burn it out.
3. To separate the chaff from the wheat.
4. To bring judgment upon those who refuse to repent.

The fire that is coming to the Church is going to burn through the structure of the Church and the exterior of our lives, to expose and reveal the deepest attitudes that lie inside the innermost recesses of our beings. Nothing will be hidden from the Spirit of God.

The true motivation of men's hearts will be revealed and the kingdom-building spirit will be destroyed!

Kingdoms are going to be torn down.

Egos of preachers are going to be torn down.

Those who have built big buildings and established ministries for the sake of promoting self are going to be removed.

I don't know about you, but I am tired of watching Christian television and hearing all these preachers talking about, "I've got the most TV stations...I've got the biggest audience...I've got the largest facility."

I'm not against building churches. They can build them as big as they want to...I really do not care. My concern is that many times when the Church gets so big, so organized, and so sophisticated, the sheep become nothing more than numbers coming in and out of buildings. As long as an individual pays his tithes and stays married to that building, he is all right.

The Church is no longer the influencing force in our cities today. It is drugs, murder, sex, and promiscuousness. What is wrong with our churches? The only thing they can get together for is some social function. Why? Kingdom-building...self...is holding us back.

We have over six billion souls in this world today. There is no way we can reach them through this kingdom-building concept of individualism...self-centeredness...where we want everything to revolve around us, our ministry, our churches.

The fire is coming! Jesus is going to visit His Church and this kingdom building spirit, this self-centeredness is going to be exposed and burnt out.

The key is repentance in an appointed season. This is God's appointed season for us to rise up, shake ourselves, and come before God in repentance.

This is Christ's message to the Church today. It is not easy. It is not a message that is going to make you jump up and down. But if you receive it as the Spirit speaks to you and act on it, it will bring you into a new level of spiritual maturity and strength.

Where Is the Fear Of The Lord?

One of the reasons the Church is in such a spiritually anemic condition, where compromise and sin have spread throughout the entire Church, is because the fear of God is missing. We have tried to bring God down to our level instead of seeking after His righteousness, walking holy before Him.

If we were walking in the fear of God today, there would be no lukewarm Christians. Knowing that God's judgments are coming upon this earth, we would not be able to sit on our comfortable pews. We would not be able to carry on "business as usual." But we would take every possible opportunity to warn others. There would be a burning fire within us, compelling us to pray...to warn...and to win the lost while there is still time.

If we were walking in the fear of God today, there would be no compromising Christians who are seeking after worldly pleasures...fulfilling the lusts of their flesh. There would not be those who are living their lives to please self instead of seeking after God and following Him in obedience.

If we were walking in the fear of God today, there would be no ungodliness, adultery, and fornication among those claiming to be born-again Christians. There would be no hypocrisy, greed, or covetousness. Instead of "sweeping it under the carpet" we would be exposing it and calling for true repentance.

Our God Is A Consuming Fire!

God is altogether holy, pure, and undefiled. Sinful flesh cannot stand in His holy Presence.

God chose to make Himself known to Moses as the God of Abraham, Isaac, and Jacob by fire. The fire represented His holiness, His glory, and His awesome power. He warned Moses not to come near, but to take off his shoes. His Presence in the flaming bush caused the surrounding ground upon which Moses stood to be holy.

What an awesome sight it was for Moses that day...to gaze into the flaming fire, see the manifested Presence of Almighty God and to hear His voice!

At the sight of the flaming fire and the sound of the voice of God, Moses trembled with fear and hid his face. God's Presence was so overwhelming, so powerful...he was afraid to even look.

In the wilderness, God instructed Moses to build an altar and to have a continual fire burning upon it, which was never to be put out. The fire was to burn continuously day and night (Leviticus 6:12-13).

This continual fire upon the altar was not an ordinary fire. It was a holy fire which came forth from God.

After Moses consecrated Aaron and his sons, anointed the tabernacle, everything in it, and the altar, they offered up the sin offering, the burnt offering, and peace offerings, as God instructed them. As they offered up these burnt offerings, God sent fire from heaven and consumed their sacrifices.

This holy fire, from God purified the sacrifices which were offered up to Him.

This holy fire, which burned continually upon the altar, is symbolic of the Holy Spirit. God has sent the fire of His Holy Spirit into our spirits. As a consuming fire, it is to continually burn within us...purging and cleansing away the sin and making us living sacrifices that are holy and acceptable to God (Romans 12:1).

Our lives are to be set on fire by the Holy Spirit, where His Presence within us is a consuming fire! As we yield to Him, this holy fire will burn away self and set us on fire with a holy burning passion for the lost. As this fire burns within us, we will walk holy before God and His power will be released in us as it was through believers in the early Church. The Spirit within us will be like a fire which cannot be contained and will not be consumed. Wherever we go, His power and glory will be manifested.

We must not be afraid of this holy fire. We must desire it...run to it!

The cry of our hearts in the days to come must be, "Oh God, consume us with Your fire! Set us on fire with your Spirit!"

Knowing that God is a consuming fire...

Knowing that Christ is coming with flaming fire to pour out God's wrath upon the wicked...

Knowing His fiery judgments are coming...

Knowing we are living in the final moments of time before Christ's return...

We must live our lives in the holy fear of the Lord! We cannot afford to be lax in our dedication and commitment to God. Neither must we allow ourselves to become complacent or so caught up with the cares of this world that we fail to prepare ourselves for that awesome day when we will stand before Him.

If you stood before Christ today, and looked into His flaming eyes of fire, what would He reveal? Would you be able to stand before Him?

We Must Shake Ourselves Out Of Our Sleep!

We cannot afford to let up in our stand against sin and begin to compromise with the world's standards.

The Church today has fallen into Satan's snare.

Christians are asleep.

Their eyes have been diverted from the goal God has given the Church to win the lost.

Their love for God has grown cold.

They are more concerned about themselves and their families than they are about winning souls and building the Kingdom of God.

Many are unwilling to pay their tithe, let alone be willing to give up all that they have to win souls into the Kingdom of God.

The majority of Christians today do not have a burning passion for souls, that would motivate them to look upon the lost in their communities and consider themselves as debtors to share with them the message of salvation. They say they believe Jesus is coming; yet they go day after day, month after month, without winning one lost soul or interceding for the lost on their jobs and in their communities.

Think about it. If we really believed Jesus is coming soon, we would not allow even one day to go by without telling someone about Jesus...without warning them of the judgment that is coming upon the earth.

Our end-time destiny in the Church is to fulfill the unfinished task God gave us of reaching the unreached masses, and evangelizing the nations before Jesus returns. Jesus said, *"and this Gospel of the Kingdom shall be preached in all the world for a witness, and then shall the end come"* (Matthew 24:14).

To meet our objective of evangelizing the world before Jesus comes, the Church must wake up from its sleep and come together as a united force with every member possessing a burning passion for the lost, and every member giving themselves in 100 percent commitment and dedication.

Are you ready to step into your end-time destiny?

The following is a special prophetic word the Lord has given me for the Church in this end-time hour. Please read it prayerfully and allow the Spirit of God to speak to your heart.

"...Oh, that My people would wake up and hear My voice! Their ears are dull from hearing. Their eyes are heavy with sleep. They have gone their own way. They sleep. They take their rest while the darkness of sin slowly surrounds them.

"Oh, that My people would wake from their sleep!

"Oh, that they would cry out to Me that I might heal their land!

"Oh, that they would see the lateness of the hour!

"My people, open your eyes! Awake from your sleep. See the signs of My coming. Do you not see? Are you too weary from the toils of this life to see? Are you too busy? Or, do you close your eyes and rest because you do not want to see?

"Why are you sleeping? I have opened your eyes. I have revealed Myself to you. I have revealed My will to you. I have shown you My power and My glory. I

have shown you My love. I have shown you My heart. Why do you close your eyes and go your own way?

"I opened your eyes that you might know Me. I opened your eyes that you would love and obey Me. I opened your eyes that you might know My heart...that you might see My love for the people who are yet in darkness. I opened your eyes to see My power and that seeing you would take My power and use it to set the captives free, to open the eyes of the blind.

"Do not close your eyes in sleep. You are My eyes upon this earth. If My people do not see and respond is there any hope for deliverance? Is there any hope for salvation?

"Open your eyes from sleep. See through My eyes the multitudes who are crying out for My mercy, for My love, for a way out of the dark pit where they have fallen.

"You are my eyes. If you fail to see and to respond, there is no hope. Those who see and do not respond, who see and do not obey, who see and turn their eyes away from those who are in darkness, I will turn away from them.

"My people, open your eyes. See Me. See My heart. See My will. Then rise up and go forth in My power. I will be with you. I will work mightily through you. Do not turn your eyes away from following after Me, from seeking to know My will. Do not get your eyes set upon the things and cares of this world. Do not get your eyes set upon yourself. See through My eyes.

"My children, I love you. I have opened your eyes that you might see Me and know Me and live. Turn not away from Me in this hour. Soon the darkness will come and there will be no more time to work. Open your eyes while there is yet time. For I have called you to be My very own. I have called you to be an extension of Myself...to open the eyes of others who are groping in darkness, without hope.

"Open your eyes out of sleep for I am coming for those who are watching, who have set their eyes upon Me and who, seeing, will obey. The hour is late. Hear My voice and open your eyes."

He that hath an ear to hear, let him hear what the Spirit is saying to His Church!

Right now, as the Presence of the Lord fills the room where you are sitting, respond to His voice. Search your heart.

Have you fallen into a spiritual sleep?

Have you been so burdened by the cares of this life that you have not been able to see the lateness of the hour?

Has your love for God and His Word grown cold?

Do you have a burning passion for lost souls?

Let us join our hearts together right now in prayer. There is no distance in prayer. As you read this prayer aloud, I am believing God to plant deep within your spirit a new vision and 100 percent dedication to Him.

"Oh God, how we praise You for speaking to us by Your Spirit! We ask You right now to shake us out of our sleep. Consume us with a burning passion, a vision of the lost. Let us see and hear the cries of lost millions in an eternity without You. Give us a world vision.

We have heard Your voice. You are calling us by Your Spirit to rise out of our sleep, out of our complacency, out of our selfishness. Forgive us. Unite us together as a powerful cohesive force...one in dedication...one in commitment and one in purpose.

We realize this is the hour You have chosen for us to go forward in Your power. We give all of ourselves to You now. Do not let us rest. Do not let us sleep. Do not allow us to grow tired. Send us forth with a new power and determination to do Your will. We will rise up and fulfill our end-time destiny!"

CHAPTER TEN

God's Destiny For His Church...Full Maturity

We are a people of destiny.

God has revealed His plan through His Word and by His Spirit.

Before the foundation of the world, He planned to have a family...a vast multitude of sons and daughters who would stand in the full stature of Jesus Christ...possessing His life, His anointing, His power and authority, His faith, His mind, His wisdom, His righteousness, His love.

At His appointed time, He gave birth to the Church. He called forth a people and breathed His Spirit upon them. He anointed them with His unlimited power and authority. He commissioned them.

Now, at His appointed time He is bringing His Church into a new position of full maturity. Jesus is saying to us through His Word:

> ...all things that I have heard of my Father I have made known unto you. Ye have not chosen me, but I have chosen you, and ordained you, that ye should go and bring forth fruit, and that your fruit should remain: that whatsoever ye shall ask of the Father in my name, he may give it you.
>
> John 15:15-16

By His Spirit, God is calling the Church to look beyond where we are today...

beyond our failures...

beyond our limitations...

beyond our man-made goals...

To see the awesome spiritual destiny He has called us to in this end time hour.

203

We are living in the time of the maturity of the fullness of the Body of Christ.

We will rise up as the strongest army of people than in any other period of the history of the world.

God is getting ready to fill us with His fullness!

He planned for this time when the Church would know no limits!

The maturity God planned for this time is coming quickly...within the next three years...and it will usher in the greatest harvest of souls in the history of the Church.

No more instability!

No more immaturity!

No more indecision!

Our spiritual destiny in these final years before Christ's return is a perfect...full-grown man...the full stature of Jesus Christ as He is today!

When we take an honest look at the level of the spiritual maturity of the Church today...with its lack of dedication and commitment, its division, self-centeredness, strife, jealousies, and other immature attitudes...it appears that we have a long way to go before we can reach full stature.

It is going to take a sovereign move of God's Spirit to bring us to this full maturity in Christ.

When we talk about the Church growing to the full stature of Jesus Christ, we are not talking about some man-made doctrine or theology.

We are not talking about some hypothetical, mystical occurrence which is going to happen some day "in the sweet by and by."

We are not talking about a high spiritual ideal that is impossible for us to reach.

Growing up to the full stature of Jesus Christ is God's plan and purpose for us today. It is God's destiny for us in this end-time hour.

It is not just a possibility...it is a reality! God will accomplish His plan and purpose in us during this Decade of Destiny!

The Church of Jesus Christ, at its current level of understanding, cannot come into this experience where we are PERFECTED...fully matured...standing in the full stature of Jesus Christ.

Something must happen!

Being changed into Christ's likeness and growing to the full stature of Jesus Christ has been considered as a goal that is either impossible for us to obtain, or that we will obtain when our bodies are changed into incorruptible bodies...into Christ's likeness...at the time of the resurrection.

There are many who teach that we will never be able to reach "perfection"...that since we are only human, it is all right to sin occasionally. They set a standard of Christian living based upon man's limitations instead of the Word of God.

Within the Body of Christ, there is such a limited vision of God's plan and purpose for His people. The vast majority of Christians today do not even know what God's eternal purpose for the Church is. They only see God's purpose as it relates to their salvation and their being raptured into heaven at the coming of Christ.

Many are at such an immature stage of spiritual growth...they are so consumed with what God can do for them, and obtaining His blessings and getting their needs met...that they cannot see God's ultimate purpose for their lives and what He wants to accomplish through them.

The Church Must Have A Fresh Vision Of Its Destiny!

Before we can move into the position of "perfection"...full spiritual maturity...that God has planned for us, the Spirit of God must so move upon us that we will receive a new fresh vision of God's eternal, ultimate intention for us today.

There is no possible way for us to grow up into the full stature of Jesus Christ until we have God's vision and clearly see His plan and purposes.

Before you can receive this revelation into your spirit, God must open your spiritual eyes so that you will be able to see beyond the limitations that have been built in your mind...beyond your limited experience...to see and know what God has planned for us in these final days before Christ's return.

Satan doesn't want the Church to reach the full stature of Jesus Christ because he knows he is defeated and fears what will happen when the Church takes its position as full grown sons of God!

The children of Israel wandered in the wilderness for forty years and eventually were defeated...disinherited and dispersed to the nations, because they lost the vision of the spiritual destiny God had called them to as His chosen people. He had planned to bless them above all other nations, and through them, to establish His will and kingdom upon the earth.

They lost the vision of their spiritual destiny, and failed to take possession of their spiritual inheritance and all the things God had prepared for them.

Within the Church today, there are very few Christians who really understand that we are living in a time of spiritual destiny, when God is going to bring to a culmination ALL that He has planned and purposed for His people. They do not realize the spiritual destiny God has called them to fulfill, and as a result, are unable to grow and develop into full maturity.

Without this vision, the Church will never be able to stand in the full stature of Jesus and operate in the same dimension of power and authority!

I pray for you right now...wherever you are...in the Name of Jesus, that God will ANOINT your spiritual eyes, that the spiritual cataracts will fall off, and that the eyes of your understanding will be opened so that you will KNOW what God has planned and purposed for your life, and that you will enter this new phase of spiritual growth, where you have reached full maturity.

God's Destiny For The Church: A "Perfect" Man

The Apostle Paul summed up the ultimate intention for the Church. He said:

> And he gave some, apostles; and some, prophets; and some, evangelists; and some, pastors and teachers; for the perfecting of the saints, for the work of the ministry, for the edifying of the body of Christ.
>
> Ephesians 4:11-12

Now, look at verses 12-13 in the Amplified version which gives a clearer understanding of the original Greek:

> His intention was the perfecting and the full equipping of the saints (His consecrated people), (that they should do) the work of ministering toward building up Christ's body (the Church), (that it might develop) until we all attain oneness in the faith and in the comprehension of the (full and accurate) knowledge of the Son of God; that (we might arrive) at really mature manhood (the completeness of personality which is nothing less than the standard height of Christ's own

perfection) the measure of the stature found in Him."

When Christ ascended into heaven, He placed the fivefold ministry within the Church for the perfecting and full equipping of the saints. Through the fivefold ministry the Church is to grow until it reaches the full stature of Jesus Christ.

The main purpose of the fivefold ministry and the reason God raised it up is to build up members within the Body of Christ until they are fully equipped to do the work of the ministry.

God has not planned for the ministry of the Church to be focused upon the pastors, teachers, evangelists, prophets, and apostles, and that they do all the work of the ministry while the other members sit back as spectators.

God never intended for the ministry of the local church to be focused solely upon the pastor who does all the preaching, teaching, and praying for the sick.

One of the major reasons for the tremendous growth in the Apostolic Church was that every believer accepted his responsibility to proclaim the Gospel, pray for the sick, cast out demons, and minister to the needs of people everywhere they went. There was no major distinction between the elders, bishops, and the other members of the Body of Christ. Every believer was a minister! If they had the gift, they were allowed to preach or teach.

It wasn't until the Church began to organize and establish a hierarchy in the Church and forbid anyone other than the bishop to preach or teach, that the growth of the Church slowed down and the Spirit began to diminish.

For more than fifty years, I have been teaching and preaching this basic truth that every born-again believer is a minister...that not just the preacher behind the pulpit is responsible for doing the work of the ministry, but every believer is called to minister in his own sphere or environment.

This truth has been the foundation of the Proof Producer message I have been preaching to more than 900,000 Nationals in the nations of the world.

Today we are seeing the Body of Christ — lay leaders and Christians around the world — taking their position as ministers...Proof Producers!

Now the time has come when God is bringing us into a new phase of spiritual strength and full maturity, where we are entering into an experience of the truth in verse 13.

Speaking of the Church, Paul said:

> *(That it might develop) until we all attain oneness in the faith and in the comprehension of the (full and accurate) knowledge of the Son of God; that (we might arrive) at really mature manhood (the completeness of personality which is nothing less than the standard height of Christ's own perfection), the measure of the stature of the fullness of the Christ, and the completeness found in Him.*
>
> Ephesians 4:13, AMP

In the King James verse it is translated, "unto a perfect man..." When Paul said we are to grow up to a "perfect man," what did he mean? What is this perfection God planned for us?

The word "perfect" in this verse is translated from the Greek word "teleios," which signifies "having reached its end"; "complete, mature, full grown, of full age."

The "perfection" Paul was referring to is the position of maturity we reach when we have come to full age...where we stand complete...full grown. This full maturity is nothing less than Christ's own perfection!

When he said we are to grow unto "a perfect man," Paul was speaking of the full maturity the whole Body of Christ is to reach in Christ, as well as the full maturity of each individual member of the Body. He said, "Till we ALL come in the unity of the faith, and of the knowledge of the Son of God."

Is It Really Possible?

God's purpose for the Church today is that we be made perfect...brought to a point of completeness in Christ where we have reached full spiritual stature...the same stature as Jesus Christ!

This is not something which we can cast aside or overlook simply because we do not understand it or because we do not feel we can reach this position as fully-matured sons of God. This "perfection" is not dependent upon our abilities or upon anything we possess, but upon His Spirit working in us to accomplish God's purposes.

I realize there are those within the Church who preach and teach it is impossible for us to ever be "perfect" in this life. And when you look at the level of spiritual experience of the majority of Christians today, including the leadership within our churches, it is easy to understand why it is hard to believe this could be possible.

In your own life, you may look at your weaknesses, failures and limitations, and think it is impossible for you to reach this place of "perfection." Not only is it possible, but God, through Christ, has made every provision for it.

God's purpose through His Word is to make us perfect...to mature and fully equip us to do His will (2 Timothy 3:16-17). One of the reasons the Church has not grown to full stature is that the vast majority of Christians have not made the Word of God a vital part in their lives. The Word has not taken root deep within their spirits.

God's purpose, through the trials and tests He allows to come into our lives, is that we be made perfect...brought to full completion...matured...full grown...lacking nothing! Instead of whining and complaining when trials come, the apostle James said we are to "count it all joy"...to rejoice, knowing that God will not only make us victorious in our trials, but through them He is working in us to perfect us (James 1:2-4). It's time for us to grow up!

In every test and every trial that we go through, God is working to strengthen us and bring us to a place of full maturity, where we are immovable and able to stand firm against every attack, and to endure every hardship in 100 percent victory!

Paul said we are to grow up into Christ "in all things." God has planned for us to grow up in the whole man...in His knowledge...in His holiness, His righteousness, and all the characteristics of Christ.

Think about it. Christ today is seated in a position of supreme power and glory at the right hand of the Father. He is a representation of what God intends us to become!

The major reason the Church today has not yet reached this position of the full stature of Jesus Christ, and the members of the Body of Christ have not taken their place as full-grown sons of God, is because we have failed to see and understand God's ultimate, eternal purpose for the Church. We must ask God to anoint our eyes so that we will have His vision.

It's Time For The Church To Grow Up!

We don't have time to get sidetracked. It's time for us to grow up...to lay aside our "childish," immature attitudes and to grow into full spiritual maturity.

Paul said:

> *When I was a child, I spake as a child, I understood as a child, I thought as a child: but when I became a man, I put away childish things.*
>
> 1 Corinthians 13:11

It's time for us to put away childish things...to put down the bottle nipple...to stop feeding only on the milk and listening to those teachings that make us feel good or appeal to our carnal nature.

If we are to grow up to the full stature of Jesus Christ, we must start digesting the "meat" of the Word that will cause us to grow strong.

It's time for us to start exercising spiritual discernment instead of following after every new doctrine that comes along. We must stop whining and complaining about how the devil is attacking us, and move to an offensive position, where we have him on the run!

As long as we remain spiritual babies...children...we cannot fulfill God's will upon the earth. It is time for us to take our position as full grown sons and daughters of God, who are a full representation of Christ to the world.

There are Christians who, although they have been saved many years, are still spiritual "babies" who have not developed their spiritual senses...their spiritual eyesight or spiritual hearing...to know what the Spirit of God is saying. They still have the bottle nipple in their mouths.

There are others who are so spiritually immature that under fire or pressure they cannot stand. When trouble comes, they can't take it and unconsciously seek to escape or run away, instead of standing and facing the enemy in the power and anointing of the Holy Spirit.

One of the greatest signs of spiritual immaturity within Christians in the Church today is the lack of discipline and commitment in their Christian walk, in their personal habits and every area of their lives. This lack of discipline is hindering the Church from growing up and it is time that we deal with it!

God's Destiny For You...Nothing Less Than The Full Stature Of Christ!

Paul said we are to grow. ...*unto a perfect man, unto the measure of the stature of the fullness of Christ* (Ephesians 4:13).

The word "measure" in this verse refers to the standard used for measuring.

In this verse, Paul gives us the standard by which we must set our goal for full maturity. He said the Church is to grow into "a perfect man"...brought to full completion...matured...full grown. But he doesn't stop there and leave us wondering what he means, or leave it to our own interpretation. He was specific. He set as the standard of measurement "the stature of the fullness of Christ."

We will not be able to reach full stature by measuring our spiritual growth by others. If we do, we will always fall short of God's ultimate intention. We cannot look at our own lives and justify our weaknesses and shortcomings because we see other Christians who are falling short of the standard God has set for us.

> *For we dare not make ourselves of the number, or compare ourselves with some that commend themselves: but they measuring themselves by themselves, and comparing themselves among themselves, are not wise.*
>
> II Corinthians 10:12

God does not want us to get our eyes on men...to put them on a pedestal and set a goal or standard to model ourselves after. There is nothing wrong with following the godly example of men and women of God who are living holy, consecrated lives. Paul told the Philippians, *"Practice what you have learned and received and heard and seen in me, and model your way of living on it..."* (Philippians 4:9, AMP).

It is good to have a godly example to learn and grow from.

However, there is only one standard we must keep as a goal before us. God's purpose is to bring us to a place of full maturity that is nothing less than the full stature of Jesus Christ.

The word "stature" in this verse is translated from a Greek word which means "Maturity." Our goal...our standard of measurement is the stature, maturity of Christ himself!

The word "fullness" is translated from the Greek word "pleroma," which "denotes fullness; that of which a thing is full." In this verse, it is used to refer to ALL Christ's virtues and attributes!

The spiritual destiny that God is bringing the Church into is "a perfect man"...brought to full completion... matured...full-grown. The standard of measurement is the stature"...maturity of the "fullness" of Christ...having all Christ's virtuous attributes.

We are to grow to the "fullness" of Christ, having...

His mind...   His faith...

His vision...   His wisdom...

His will...   His righteousness...

His consecration... His holiness...

His anointing...   His love...

His power and authority...

His glory...

ALL that He has and is!

God's Destiny For You...The fullness Of The Godhead!

In Christ, dwells all the "fullness" of the Godhead. Paul described that "fullness" to the Colossians. He said:

(Now) He is the exact likeness of the unseen God

(the visible representation of the invisible; He is the First-born) of all creation.

Colossians 1:15, AMP

In Christ, all the divine fullness dwells:

For it has pleased (the Father) that all the divine fullness (the sum total of the divine perfection, powers and attributes) should dwell in Him permanently.

Colossians 1:19, AMP

The "fullness" that is in Christ is the Godhead in the totality of His power and attributes. It is the complete fullness and perfection of the divine essence of God.

Paul said:

For in Him the whole fullness of the Deity (the Godhead), continues to dwell in bodily form (giving complete expression of the divine nature). And you are in Him, made full and have come to fullness of life (in Christ you too are filled with the Godhead: Father, Son and Holy Spirit, and reach full spiritual stature). And He is the Head of all rule and authority (of every angelic principality and power).

Colossians 2:9-10, AMP

The "fullness" of the Godhead dwells in Christ, and because Christ dwells within us, we are also filled with the "fullness" of the Godhead...Father, Son, and Holy Spirit!

The Godhead lives within us!

The key to reaching the full stature of Jesus Christ is our union with Christ. Paul said, "in Him" we are filled with the Godhead and reach full spiritual stature. We must remain IN HIM...vitally united to Him through a continual communion and relationship with Him.

IN HIM, we have the very life-flow of God in all His power and glory manifested within us!

215

IN HIM, we have His very nature and His divine attributes imparted to us by His Spirit!

We become partakers of His divine nature! (2 Peter 1:4)

IN HIM, we have everything and are able to grow up in everything into Him! Paul said we are to "grow up into him in all things, which is the head, even Christ" (Ephesians 4:15). This means we are to GROW UP in the whole man...in knowledge...righteousness...holiness and ALL the characteristics of Christ.

This growth is the RESULT of our union with Him. As we grow in our relationship and union with Him, the more we grow into His stature...the more we have His nature imparted to us...the more His life is formed and manifested in us.

God's Destiny For You...The Express Image Of Christ!

God's ultimate intention is that through our union with Christ, we will be transformed into his image...whereby we are a full manifestation and representation of Him to the world.

Just as Jesus Christ, in the form of human flesh, was the express image of God, God has planned for you and me, in the form of human flesh, to be the express image of Christ now...here on this earth!

God planned that, through Christ's death and resurrection, many sons would be born who would be the express image of their elder Brother, Jesus Christ, and would become joint-heirs with Him.

Paul said:

For whom he did foreknow, he also did predestinate to be conformed to the image of his

Son, that he might be the first-born among many brethren.

Romans 8:29

The word "conformed" in this verse is translated from a Greek word which means "to bring to the same outward expression as something else."

God has planned for you to be brought to the same expression...the same image of Jesus Christ as He is now!

The word "image," translated from the Greek word "eikon" is used to refer to believers in being a representation of what God is. It does not mean merely resembling Christ, but representing Him, we are to represent Him, not something like Him, but what He is in all his glory!"

In writing to the Colossians, Paul described Jesus as being *"...the image of the invisible God"* (Colossians 1:15). He was a visible representation and manifestation of God.

While Jesus lived His life on this earth as the Son of God in the form of human flesh, he was the exact image...the visible representation and manifestation of God to men.

To see Jesus was to see God.

Jesus said, *"...he that seeth me seeth him that sent me"* (John 12:45).

When Philip asked Jesus to show them the Father, Jesus told him,

...Have I been so long time with you, and yet hast thou not known me, Philip? he that hath seen me hath seen the Father; and how sayest thou then, Shew us the Father?

John 14:9

When Jesus told Philip, "He that hath seen me hath seen the Father," He was not referring to His own outward, physical appearance...His eyes, nose, hands, and feet. Jesus was referring to the life of God that proceeded forth from

His innermost being. As the Son of God, the life of God the Father flowed through Him...healing the sick, casting out demons, forgiving sins...as a visible manifestation of God to the world.

As Jesus was a visible representation of God to men on this earth, you are to be a visible representation and manifestation of Christ to men on earth today.

By His Spirit, God is conforming you into the express image of Christ. I realize this may be hard for you to understand...how that you, with all your human limitations, can be changed into Christ's same image, where you have grown up unto His full stature.

The disciples didn't understand how Jesus, a man with whom they walked, talked and lived, could be an outward manifestation of God. Jesus said, "Look at Me, Philip. When you've seen Me, you've seen God."

It was not Jesus' physical features that were the exact image of God. And it is not your physical features that are being changed into Christ's image. It is your spirit...where Christ lives within you. It is your inner man that is growing up into the full stature of Jesus Christ.

Through the power of the Holy Spirit working within you, your inner man is continually being changed and transformed. As you begin to see Christ as He is and know Him in His fullness, you are being changed into His image from one degree of glory to another.

God's Destiny For You...A Full Manifestation Of Christ To The World!

Even before the foundation of the world, in the Father heart of God, He desired to have a people...sons and daughters...who would bear His image, His likeness...who would share His very life, His nature, His purpose, His vision, and be fully conformed to His will!

Paul told the Ephesians:

Blessed be the God and Father of our Lord Jesus Christ, who hath blessed us with all spiritual blessings in heavenly places in Christ: According as he hath chosen us in him before the foundation of the world, that we should be holy and without blame before him in love: Having predestinated us unto the adoption of children by Jesus Christ to himself, according to the good pleasure of his will, To the praise of the glory of his grace, wherein he hath made us accepted in the beloved.

Ephesians 1:3-6

Before the foundation of the world, "according to the good pleasure of His will," God planned for the "adoption" of children through Jesus Christ. He desired to have a people through whom He would manifest His power and glory to the world.

This is your spiritual destiny and mine, and He will accomplish it in this end time hour!

The time has come for us to grow up...to take our position as fully-matured sons and daughters of God!

Through our relationship and union with Christ, we are God's children, joint-heirs of all that the Father has. However, as long as we remain children... spiritual babies... we will be unable to take our position as sons who are entitled to full rights and privileges of the Kingdom of God.

Paul told the Galatians:

Now I say, That the heir, as long as he is a child, differeth nothing from a servant, though he be lord of all; But is under tutors and governors until the time appointed of the father. Even so we, when we were children, were in bondage under the elements of the world: But when the fullness of the time was come, God

*sent forth his Son, made of a woman, made under the
law, to redeem them that were under the law, that we
might receive the adoption of sons. And because ye are
sons, God hath sent forth the Spirit of His Son into your
hearts, crying, Abba, Father. Wherefore thou art no more
a servant, but a son; and if a son, then an heir of God
through Christ.*

Galatians 4:1-7

According to Hebrew custom among prominent
families, it was the practice of the father to place his infant
son under the care and training of a trusted
servant. The child was entrusted into the care of this
servant or tutor for maturing and discipline until the time
he would come of age.

The child, though he was an heir to all that his father
owned, was no different than the servants. He was raised
alongside the servant's children. They played and ate together.
There was no difference between them until that child grew
to maturity. During this period of training and preparation for
full sonship, it was the tutor's job to teach the child and bring
him into the ways, purposes, and spirit of the father.

Then at the time when the child had reached full maturity, the father, through adoption, placed his son in full
sonship privileges. According to Jewish tradition, this usually
occurred at the age of thirty. During a time of celebration,
the son was acknowledged and the father announced, "This
is my son, in whom I am well pleased."

The word "adoption" is translated from the Greek word
"huiothesia," which means "placing as a son." This adoption did
not involve placing a child outside the family into a new family.
"Adoption" in the Bible was the placing of one who was already
a child into full sonship rights. At that time, he was entitled to
the inheritance of the name of the family he was born into.

By his birth, he was a child, a legal heir, but preparation and discipline brought him to adoption and the full stature of sonship.

This is the time appointed by the Father for the Church to rise up to full stature! The time has come for our adoption... when God places His vast family of full-grown sons into FULL sonship rights and privileges and we take possession of all that He has provided for us. It is not a matter of whether we can or will reach this position of full stature...

It is not a matter of our natural abilities or our efforts...

By his spirit, He is bringing the Church to full stature! We will reach this position where we are full-grown... where we are a full representation and manifestation of Christ to the world.

How Can I Attain The Full Stature Of Jesus Christ?

How limited we have been in our spiritual vision of the purpose of the Holy Spirit in our lives! The concept many Christians have concerning the work and ministry of the Holy Spirit is that He has been sent to bless them. They have failed to go beyond the point of blessing. Others have sought only after the power...the gifts...the manifestations of the Holy Spirit.

We cannot stand in the full stature of Jesus Christ, and operate under the same power and anointing, until the Holy Spirit has accomplished His work in bringing us to full maturity.

We have received the Holy Spirit...the Spirit of adoption...for the purpose of bringing us to full stature...to full-grown manhood as sons of God. Just as in the Hebrew custom the child was placed under a tutor to teach, train, discipline, and bring him into the ways, purposes, and spirit of the father; God has placed the Spirit within us to teach us

His ways, to lead us into all truth (John 16:13), to reveal Christ to us, to mold and transform us into the same image as Jesus Christ.

Although we are His sons and are heirs of God and joint-heirs with Christ, we cannot take full possession of our spiritual inheritance as His sons, until we have been brought by his spirit to full maturity. Paul said the true sons of God are those who are led by His Spirit, who are yielded to and controlled by the Spirit.

As you look at the level of where you are in your spiritual growth, you may be thinking... "Brother Cerullo, HOW is it possible for me to grow up to the full stature of Jesus Christ?"

"What can I do to reach this position as a full-grown son of God?"

There is no spiritual maturity apart from Christ. We grow as we remain in vital union and communion with Him, where we are drawing upon His life within us. Our growth is the result of a continuous work of the Holy Spirit in our lives.

Our total dependence must be upon the Holy Spirit, to teach, train, and discipline us, until we reach the full stature of Jesus Christ. There is absolutely no way possible for us to reach full stature through our own human efforts.

Paul wrote to the Galatians, who were striving through their own efforts to fulfill the law instead of walking by faith. He said:

> *Are you so foolish and so senseless and so silly? Having begun (your new life spiritually) with the (Holy) Spirit, are you now reaching perfection (by dependence) on the flesh?*
>
> Galatians 3:3, AMP

We cannot reach the full stature of Jesus Christ through a dependence upon our natural abilities... through our striving to be like Jesus. If we try in our own efforts, we are only deceiving ourselves, and we will fail.

In the spiritual realm, when an individual is born again, it is not necessary for him to struggle to make himself grow to full maturity. He cannot, in his own strength, cause himself to grow to the full stature of Jesus Christ.

The life and the power to bring us to full maturity is in the "seed" of the Father which is in us. The life, nature, and the characteristics of the Father are in the seed.

Jesus was begotten of the Father, conceived by the Holy Spirit. Over two thousand years ago, the Holy Spirit came upon a virgin named Mary and implanted the incorruptible seed of Jesus Christ within her womb. That holy seed grew and in the fullness of time, Christ, the Son of God, was born.

Just as Jesus the Son of God, was conceived by the Holy Spirit in Mary's womb, the very life of Jesus Christ was conceived in you by the Holy Spirit.

Peter said:

> *Being born again, not of corruptible seed, but of incorruptible, by the word of God, which liveth and abideth forever.*
>
> I Peter 1:23

You have been born again by an incorruptible seed, and it is through that seed that Christ's life will be manifested in your life.

The Power Is In The Incorruptible Seed!

Man does not possess the power or right to become a son of God. No man can even come to Christ unless the Spirit of God draws him (John 6:44). You didn't just decide one day to accept Jesus Christ as your Savior. By His Spirit, He drew you.

Then, when you responded to the drawing of the Holy Spirit and surrendered your entire being to Christ, you were given the power...the rightful claim...to become a son of God.

The life...the incorruptible seed...that is in you was born of God. You were begotten by the Father.

"Of his own will begat he us with the word of truth, that we should be a kind of firstfruits of his creatures" (James 1:18).

The word "begat" in this verse means "to give birth to; to bring forth." By the exercising of His own will, God the Father gave you birth. You were born again, not by your own will, but by the will of God (John 1:13).

Because that incorruptible seed remains within you, it will produce the life and nature of Christ within you. The apostle John said,

> *No one who is born of God will continue to sin, because God's seed remains in him; he cannot go on sinning, because he has been born of God.*
>
> 1 John 3:9, NIV

The power to change and conform you into Christ's image is in the incorruptible seed!

The power for you to be perfected...brought to full maturity, where you are a full-grown son of God, is in the incorruptible seed!

The power for you to grow up to the full stature of Jesus Christ is in the incorruptible seed!

That is why Christ said, *"Be ye therefore perfect, even as your Father which is in heaven is perfect"* (Matthew 5:48).

His seed remains in you, producing His life and causing you to grow to His full stature.

Christ's life grows and develops into full stature as you nourish that life within you and as you are fully yielded to the Holy Spirit. Just as a baby cannot grow to an adult without proper food and nourishment, neither can the incorruptible seed within you grow and reach full stature unless it receives proper nourishment.

In order for you to grow and develop until you reach full stature, you must remain vitally united to Christ, where His life is flowing into you...where you are not only feeding on the "strong meat" of the Word, but where you are also applying the Word in your life and are walking in obedience to Him. Jesus said,

> *Abide in me, and I in you. As the branch cannot bear fruit of itself, except it abide in the vine; no more can ye, except ye abide in me.*
>
> John 15:4

We Are Changed And Conformed Into The Image Of Christ By His Spirit.

Paul said:

> *But we all, with open face beholding as in a glass the glory of the Lord, are changed into the same image from glory to glory, even as by the spirit of the Lord.*
>
> 2 Corinthians 3:18

Just as in Hebrew tradition tutors were placed over the child to teach, train, discipline, and bring him to a place of maturity, where he had been conformed to the mind, will and purposes of his father, so God has placed His Spirit within us to teach, train, and discipline us until we reach full maturity in Christ.

It is by his spirit that God reveals Himself and His will to us. Paul said,

Now we have received, not the spirit of the world, but the spirit which is of God; that we might know the things that are freely given to us of God.

I Corinthians 2:12

It is His Spirit Who reveals Christ in all His fullness and joins us together with Him as one! It is His Spirit Who leads and guides us into all truth!

It is His Spirit Who manifests and releases God's power and anointing within us to work the works of God!

It is His Spirit Who manifests the fruit of the Spirit and the gifts in our lives!

It is His Spirit working within us that enables us to walk in victory over all the power of the enemy!

To grow to full stature, we must be sensitive to the leading of the Holy Spirit. We must be careful not to grieve or quench the flow of His Spirit, but allow Him full control to accomplish His work in bringing us to full stature.

Paul said, *"For as many as are led by the Spirit of God, they are the sons of God"* (Romans 8:14). Only as we are yielded to and obedient to the Holy Spirit, will we be able to grow to full stature.

We grow and reach the full stature of Jesus Christ as we grow in a full and accurate knowledge of Him. If our vision or revelation of Him is limited, or our comprehension of Who He really is not strong, our spiritual growth will be limited.

God's Destiny For His Church...
Unity In The Spirit!

As God brings the Church into full maturity, we will also enter into the unity Jesus prayed would happen.

One of the major signs of spiritual immaturity within the Church is a lack of unity. The Apostle Paul considered the believers in the Corinthian Church as spiritual babies, who could only drink milk because there was strife and divisions among them.

He said:

> *For ye are yet carnal: for whereas there is among you envying, and strife, and divisions, are ye not carnal, and walk as men?*
>
> I Corinthians 3:3

The time has come for the Church to take the mask off. We are not the powerful, united force God intended for us to be!

The Church has failed to produce unity!

Since the birth of the Church, men have tried to produce unity, but they have failed. As early as 325 A.D., an Ecumenical Council of church bishops was formed under Constantine the Emperor and convened in Nicaea in an effort to bring unity within the Body of Christ.

Today we are disjointed...divided. The time has come for the Body to grow to full maturity, where all the members of the Body are functioning together... united together in the Spirit.

Each denomination is functioning individually as a separate organism with its own set of goals, needs, and problems. Each denomination's major concern is its own progress and welfare. Within the denomination itself there are major conflicts and factions dividing it.

At the local level, we see the same principle repeated. Most local churches today are so totally engrossed in their own efforts, problems, and ministering to the needs within their own church body, that they very seldom consider how they are fitting together with other members of the Body of Christ.

Within the churches, smaller groups or factions are operating which are more concerned with doing things their way than they are of keeping unity within the Church. There is envy and strife among members...long-standing feuds...members refusing to talk with one another... rebellion against pastors and church leaders. Pastors are jealous of other pastors...there is criticism concerning television evangelists...and on and on.

Within our homes, where is the peace and unity? God designed the unity of the family to be a model of the unity we are to experience in the Church. There can be no unity in the Church until there is unity at home.

In our families we have our differences. We have our own ideas and separate personalities. That isn't going to change. But, if we cannot walk together in love and unity in our homes...husbands with their wives, parents with their children, children with one another...how are we going to be able to walk in unity in our churches?

A large majority of Christians today are living and operating in their own little world, where they are so absorbed in developing their own spiritual lives and building their own ministries, they fail to be concerned with how they are building up and edifying the Body of Christ. There are many Christians who are still living their lives according to their own wills, fulfilling their own desires; instead of living vitally united to Christ, fulfilling His will.

The Early Church experienced the same types of difficulties and divisions we are experiencing today. In the Corinthian church there was envying, strife, and division. the members had separated themselves into groups. Some were saying, "I follow Paul," others were saying, "I follow Apollos...I follow Cephas...I follow Christ" (1 Corinthians 1:12). There was strife among the members, with members taking one another to court.

Does this sound familiar?

There were members who magnified their own spiritual gifts and powers to depreciate those of other members. There were disputes about the value of spiritual gifts and how to regulate them in the church. There were bitter arguments regarding the question of eating meats offered to idols.

In the Philippian church, Euodias and Syntyche (two leading Christian women in the church) were having personality clashes, causing division within the Body (Philippians 4:2). Members within the church were filled with pride and vainglory, which also proved to be a source of division. Some of the members were more concerned with having their opinions and groups established and promoted, than unity being preserved within the church.

Within the church in Rome there were differences of opinion regarding what was lawful to eat and what wasn't, and differences concerning what religious days to observe.

When Paul wrote to the Corinthians, he said,

> ...I could not address you as spiritual but as worldly - mere infants in Christ. I gave you milk, not solid food, for you were not yet ready for it. Indeed, you are still not ready. You are still worldly. For since there is jealousy and quarreling among you, are you not worldly? Are you not acting like mere men?
>
> 1 Corinthians 3:1-3, NIV

As Long As Divisions Remain, We Are Babies!

The Body of Christ will never function as the mature, full-grown Body of Christ until we, as individual members, have an experience where we begin to recognize God has joined us together and begin walking together as ONE...united in the Spirit.

Until then, we will be spiritual babies needing to be fed with milk!

As long as there is strife, envy, and divisions within the Body, we are babies...we are carnal and cannot reproduce the life and power of God intended for us to demonstrate to the world.

Throughout the centuries, ecumenical leaders from various denominations throughout the church world...Catholics, Lutherans, Reformed, Methodists, Anglicans, Presbyterians, Baptists, Pentecostals, and Evangelicals ...have met together in councils and committees in an attempt to reach unity in doctrine and church order, as a means of merging and uniting together.

The unity God planned for the Church to experience will not be produced by men's futile attempts. It will not be produced by merging denominations. Since the birth of the Church, Christians have had different methodologies, ideas, and doctrinal differences.

The place where we can be one is not on the surface. It's not in methodology. It's not in ideology or doctrine.

The place where we can be one is in Jesus. There can be no unity without Him. He is the Head of the Church. As we are joined together in an intimate relationship with Him, we are joined together with one another and we become one with Him.

The time has come for you and me to look beyond the idiosyncrasies of our brothers and sisters. It is time for us to get our eyes off methodologies, people's mannerisms, and our differences. We must realize there is a place where we can be one, without losing our identities.

Unity is a spiritual force produced by the Spirit!

The type of unity I am talking about is not a vague spiritual generality. It is not an ethereal concept. It is a spiritual, life-giving force, produced by the Spirit of the living God!

As the Church grows up and comes into the position of full maturity God has planned, Christ's prayer for unity will come to pass. The true Body of Christ will now enter into the unity Jesus prayed would happen.

We will be united! Not in all our theology. Not in our methodologies. A spirit of unity is coming to the Church that will make us one and forget our labels. It won't matter whether a believer is Baptist, Catholic, Assembly of God, Methodist, or any other denomination.

The labels will be put aside and we will be united around two things...

our vision for the lost and our love for God!

One of God's major purposes in the end-time outpouring of the Holy Spirit, is to bring the Church into full maturity...where we have been molded and conformed into one united body...where we are a full representation and manifestation of Christ in all His Being!

Following a great sifting that is coming in the Church, producing holiness, there will be a move of the Spirit bringing the Body of Christ together in true unity.

Members of the Body of Christ will come together in a new relationship, where we are walking in close covenant relationship with one another...where we will be closer to each other than we are to our own flesh and blood. In this new covenant relationship, we will realize that our true family are those who have been united together in the Spirit.

Before the Church can enter into this experience, where we are fully mature and functioning at the full capacity God intended for us, we must first come into a new relationship of true unity. We must have a fresh manifestation...a dynamic move of the Holy Spirit that will lift us up from where we are and set us on a higher spiritual plateau.

A mighty, fiery move of the Holy Spirit is going to sweep throughout the Church...in North America, Europe, the West Indies, the Philippines, Latin America, Africa, Indonesia, Malaysia...around the world! The Holy Spirit is going to melt our hearts and make us yielded and submissive in the hands of God. By His Spirit working within us, we will be molded into one body!

When this happens...when we become ONE, united in the Spirit...get ready! The world will see the greatest release of the miracle power of God through the Church it has ever seen. We will be living, walking manifestations of the miracle power of God to the world!

Unity in the Spirit is the key to the release of the power of God within the Church! It is the key to walking in the fullness of Christ.

This unity that is coming to the Church is not on the surface. It is not an outward manifestation of various denominations and church organizations uniting together, adhering to certain rules, and coming into agreement on various doctrines and methods of worship. The unity God has planned for us to experience is not a manmade unity...it is a spiritual unity.

We Are One Body!

Jesus, knowing that He was going to be crucified and that the early Church would face intense persecution after He was gone, prayed for the Church that they would be united into one, just as He and the Father are one.

He prayed:

> *...Holy Father, keep through thine own name those whom thou hast given me, that they may be one, as we are. That they all may be one; as thou, Father, art in me, and I in thee, that they also may be one in us: that the world may believe that thou hast sent me.*
>
> John 17:11, 21

The Church today is to experience the same unity that Christ has with the Father. Jesus is one with the Father. They are vitally united together by the Spirit. He and the Father are eternally bound together with divine love. Their wills are blended into One. Jesus said, *"My meat is to do the will of him that sent me, and to finish his work"* (John 4:34). He said, *"I and my Father are one"* (John 10:30). *"The Father is in me, and I in him"* (John 10:38).

The Church is to have this same type of spiritual unity with one another. We are to be vitally united together in a covenant relationship by the same Spirit, possessing the same divine, self-sacrificing love, our minds and wills blended in harmony with the will of God.

In Christ, we are one body, joined together by the same spirit. In God's eyes there aren't hundreds of different churches separated into denominations; there is only one Body!

Paul told the Ephesians,

> *There is one body, and one Spirit, even as ye are called in one hope of your calling; One Lord, one faith, one baptism, One God and Father of all, who is above all, and through all, and in you all.*
>
> Ephesians 4:4-6

We must recognize that we are already one. We are not going to be one sometime in the future. We are one in God's eyes, right now. We are baptized by one Spirit into one body.

There isn't one Spirit for the Baptists, another Spirit for the Methodists, and another for the Pentecostal! We are joined together by the same Spirit. There is only one Spirit and it is the uniting force within the Body of Christ.

It is time for the Church to grow up in its understanding and comprehension of what is intended for the Church to be. Because we have not been able to see the Body of Christ as God sees us, we have allowed strife, bitterness, suspicion, envy, and pride to divide us. We have failed to manifest God's love to one another.

The time has come for the Church to get rid of the suspicion and strife. We must:

Stop looking at our differences...

Stop competing...

Stop criticizing and tearing down one another!

We are Christ's BODY! WE are not a product of man's organization. Members of this sacred body have been born again by the Spirit of God, and have been made part of His living Body!

We have not joined an organization...we have been birthed into His divine Body!

As His Body upon this earth, we are to function together and be a full manifestation of Christ, ministering in the same capacity as He did while He was in a physical body upon this earth.

We are not a lot of different organizations or bodies functioning separately...we are one Body. Paul told the Romans,

> *So we, numerous as we are, are one body in Christ (the Messiah), and individually we are parts one of another (mutually dependent on one another).*
>
> Romans 12:5, AMP

As members of Christ's Body, we are joined together with one another in a sacred bond that transcends flesh and blood.

As members of His divine body, we share the same life...His life flows through us, making us One.

We have been baptized by his spirit into one body. Paul told the Corinthians:

> *And now there are (certainly) many limbs and organs, but a single body.*
>
> 1 Corinthians 12:20, AMP

He said,

> *Now you (collectively) are Christ's Body and (individually) you are members of it, each part severally and distinct (each with his own place and*

function).

1 Corinthians 12:27, AMP

God's ultimate intention for us is that we grow together...that we fully develop and mature until we reach our full stature as the Body of Christ, manifesting all the fullness of Christ's glory and power.

Jesus prayed:

> *And the glory which thou gavest me I have given them; that they may be one, even as we are one: I in them, and thou in me, that they may be made perfect in one...*

John 17:22-23

God planned for the Body of Christ to grow together until we all become united, in the Spirit, into one body...into a perfect man...which is nothing less than Christ's own perfection.

He planned for every member of Christ's Body to be One with Christ. And, as they remain continually in Him, they grow and develop in their knowledge and experience in Christ until they are perfected ...fully mature, conformed, and transformed...by His Spirit, into Christ's image.

As the Body of Christ grows together in the knowledge of Jesus Christ, with each member filling his place within the Body...building and edifying the Body in love...the Body grows and matures until it reaches full maturity as the One living, powerful Body of Christ!

As the Church begins to experience a true manifestation of God's love and unity in the Spirit, we will see the greatest manifestation of God's miracle power the world has ever seen!

As the world sees the members of the Body of Christ, walking together in the unity of the Spirit, they will know that Christ is Who He claims to be.

235

They will KNOW that He came from the Father and they will KNOW and experience the same love the Father has for His son!

God Has An End Time Destiny For You!

Are you tired of living below your rights and privileges as a full grown son or daughter of God Almighty?

Are you tired of relying upon your natural strength and natural mind?

Are you hungry for an experience of the unlimited, true power of Pentecost?

Do you really desire to be used by God in this end-time hour?

God destined you to be a man or woman of power and authority, through whom His unlimited power flows in a full manifestation!

God destined you, through Christ, to be a son or daughter of God possessing full rights of sonship as a joint heir with Christ!

God destined you to be perfected and fully equipped to do His work!

God destined you to be anointed and empowered by the Holy Spirit...the Third Person of the Trinity living within you!

God destined you to have 100 percent victory over 100 percent of the enemy, 100 percent of the time!

God destined you to be conformed into the image of Christ where you are a full representation of Him to the world!

God destined you to have a divine capability to do the same works Jesus did and greater!

God destined you to be a living witness giving undeniable proof that Jesus is the Son of God by the miracle-working power flowing out of your life!

God destined you to no longer live according to a natural power, but according to a supernatural power imparted by the indwelling of the Holy Spirit!

God destined you to be perfected and grow up to full maturity into the full stature of Jesus Christ!

God destined that you be filled with the fullness of the Godhead: Father, Son, and Holy Spirit!

God destined that you be baptized by one Spirit into one Body and walk in unity in the Spirit.

My question to you is...

"How far do you want to go?"

The Key...Power Intimacy!

To step into God's end-time destiny, you must go beyond the limitations of your natural mind and receive a revelation of all that God has planned for His Church in this hour.

Head knowledge is not enough!

By His Spirit, God must take you beyond your limited understanding, beyond your limitations, beyond head knowledge into an experience where He releases this revelation into your spirit.

Unless you receive a revelation, this message will just touch your natural mind. It is my prayer that God will release a full revelation of the destiny He has for you.

To step into your end time destiny you must have a fresh revelation of Christ as He is today. When your spiritual eyes are opened and you see Him clearly, you will receive the power that the early Church experienced.

The ministry of the Holy Spirit is to reveal and manifest Christ to you. Jesus said that when the Holy Spirit comes to live within you, He will be His Representative. The Holy Spirit will reveal all that He is and all that He has. He said,

All things that the Father hath are mine:

237

therefore said I, that he shall take of mine, and shall shew it unto you.

John 16:15

The more revelation we have of Christ through the Holy Spirit, the more we will be changed and transformed into His likeness. John wrote:

Beloved, now are we the sons of God, and it doth not yet appear what we shall be: but we know that, when he shall appear, we shall be like him; for we shall see him as he is. And every man that hath this hope in him purifieth himself, even as he is pure.

1 John 3:2-3

We grow and are changed into His image as we see Him...as we have a revelation of Him in all His power and glory, yield ourselves fully to His Spirit working within us and walk in obedience to what He has revealed in His Word.

Paul told the Corinthian Church,

But we all, with open face beholding as in a glass the glory of the Lord, are changed into the same image from glory to glory, even as by the Spirit of the Lord.

2 Corinthians 3:18

Do you want to take your position in this end-time hour as a full-grown child of God possessing full sonship rights and privileges?

Do you want God's unlimited power flowing unhindered through your life to heal the sick, cast out demons, and proclaim the Gospel in a demonstration of power?

Get into the Presence of the Lord. Don't seek after power...seek Him. Seek after Christ and to know Him in His fullness. Seek to be filled with a "full knowledge" of Him.

There is only one way you will be able to fulfill the destiny God has for your life...through an intimate communion and fellowship with Christ. I am not talking about a casual relationship, but an intimate relationship you have nurtured and developed through prayer...waiting before Him in His Presence...meditating upon His Word...listening for His voice...walking circumspectly before Him... following His direction...fulfilling His will.

Jesus said,

> *The person who has My commands and keeps them is the one who (really) loves Me, and whoever (really) loves Me will be loved by My Father. And I (too) will love him and will show (reveal, manifest) Myself to Him (I will let Myself be clearly seen by him and make myself real to him).*

John 14:21, AMP

The type of relationship God plans for us to have with Christ is the same relationship Christ has with the Father. Jesus said, *"I and my Father are one"* (John 10:30).

He said, *"Believe me that I am in the Father, and the Father in me"* (John 14:11).

> *...The Son can do nothing of himself, but what he seeth the Father do: for what things soever he doeth, these also doeth the Son likewise.*

John 5:19

> *...I do nothing of myself; but as my Father hath taught me, I speak these things.*

John 8:28

It is through this intimacy, whereby we have a relationship where He is in us and we are vitally united to Him, that His life and power are released in us. We cannot produce the power of God through our efforts. God's power is released as a result of our relationship. You will be able to grow to the full stature of Jesus Christ and be conformed into His image through your relationship with Christ.

This relationship I am talking about is power intimacy.

Power, which is the promise of the Holy Spirit, does not travel in words.

Speaking is not enough. You can speak the Word and talk it all you want, but it will not produce power.

When are we going to get the mask off?

Power doesn't travel in words. It travels in relationship. When you get on your face before the Lord, and the Holy Spirit begins to open your eyes and reveal Christ to you, something begins to happen to you. You come to the place of full surrender where, like Paul, you say, *"I am crucified with Christ: nevertheless I live; yet not I, but Christ liveth in me"* (Galatians 2:20).

Not until you come to this place in your relationship with Christ where you are willing to die to self will you experience the power of God flowing through you as it did through the disciples in the early Church.

Jesus said,

> *...Except a corn of wheat fall into the ground and die, it abideth alone: but if it die, it bringeth forth much fruit.*
>
> John 12:24

Power travels in relationship.

The 120 disciples in the Early Church did not receive the promised baptism of the Holy Spirit on the first day...the second...or the ninth day. It took ten days.

Why did they have to wait?

God was working things out in their lives... changing them...emptying them of self...bringing them into a position to receive.

Is it any wonder that Paul, as he approached the end of his life and ministry cried, *"That I may know him, and the power of his resurrection, and the fellowship of his sufferings..."* (Philippians 3:10).

Church, Rise Up...Step Into Your Destiny!

How hungry are you for a full manifestation of Christ in your life?

Are you hungry enough to make a new dedication of yourself...everything you are and everything you have?

Are you ready for God to give you a breakthrough that will take you beyond every natural limitation, every doubt, every hindrance; into an experience where you are moving into His end-time destiny for your life?

The word "breakthrough" means "a sudden burst of advanced knowledge that takes us past a line of defense."

The key to your breakthrough is timing. It is knowing God's timing, knowing what He has planned to do, and acting in faith upon what He reveals.

This is God's time for His Church to grow into full maturity. He is getting ready to fill us with His fullness!

There has been a wall of resistance. There have been things in the spirit that we have not understood. But, I prophesy to you that God's Church will make spiritual breakthroughs. Spiritual Knowledge is increasing that breaks through the resistance.

Now is God's time for the Church to get advanced knowledge through the Holy Spirit, to tap into the very mind of God, and to experience a supernatural manifestation taking us into the fullness of all that He has planned for us in this end-time hour before Jesus comes.

Receive the Word of prophecy God gave me for this great end-time move of His Spirit. Please do not take this Word lightly. Read it carefully and prayerfully. Then respond to what the Spirit of God is saying to you.

"Rise up! Rise up, My people. Take your position as My Body. This is the hour I have ordained for you to be strong and mighty in battle. This is the hour I have ordained for you to manifest My glory throughout the nations of the earth."

"Open your eyes and look around you. The land lies barren and desolate before you. The darkness of sin and corruption covers the face of the earth. The people are in bondage. There is pain, sickness, and despair."

"Rise up! Rise up! Come together. Unite your hearts together as one. Be of one mind and one spirit. There is much for you to do. The days are yet coming when an even greater darkness shall surround you. But, in that hour of darkness My glory shall be upon you."

"In that day you shall not be weak or fearful, for you shall know that I am in your midst. You shall know that I have called you from the ends of the earth and joined you together as My chosen people...My Church... My Body...My Bride."

"Rise up! Awake to the power I have placed within you. Awake to the purpose for which I have called you. Take your place wherein I have called and placed you in My Body. Be faithful. Be obedient. Walk together as one."

"Rise up! Walk in unity. Walk in My love. Recognize I have joined you together. You are one together with Me. It is My will that you rise up in this hour...that you take your place at My side as joint-heirs in My Father's kingdom."

"All those who hear My Word and hearken unto Me in this hour and obey, will receive a refreshing of My Spirit and will walk in the fullness of My power."

"Even as a mighty army preparing for battle, I say unto you, rise up...take your position...the battle is at hand!"

"But KNOW the victory is yours...and you shall eat and enjoy (have to use at your pleasure) the spoils of the heritage I planned and prepared for you."

Rise up, Church!

Take your position...

Step into your end-time destiny!

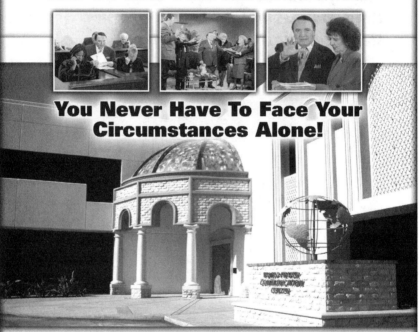

WORLD PRAYER CENTER

MIRACLES HAPPEN WHEN SOMEONE CARES...
AND WE CARE WHAT HAPPENS TO YOU!

You Never Have To Face Your Circumstances Alone!

Call if you need healing, restoration in your marriage, financial breakthrough, deliverance from alcohol, drugs, or other addictions. Your phone is your point of contact.

Our trained intercessors are ready to pray and believe God for the miracle you need!

• Prayer Help Line
• Trained, anointed intercessors. Only qualified, trained intercessors will be on the phone lines
• Non-denominational: We encourage Catholics, Protestants, Jews, people of all faiths to call

There is no distance in prayer!

CALL THE MORRIS CERULLO PRAYER HELP LINE

1-858-HELPLINE

helpline@mcwe.com
Fax: 858-427-0555

435-7546

Brother Cerullo,

Please place my requests on the Miracle Prayer Altar and pray for these needs:

_____

_____

_____

_____

_____

_____

❑ Enclosed is my love gift of $(£)_____ to help you win souls and to support this worldwide ministry.

❑ Please tell me how I can become a God's Victorious Army member...to help you reach the nations of the world, and receive even more anointed teaching on a monthly basis!

Name _____

Address _____

City _____ State or Province _____

Postal Code _____ Phone Number (____)_____

E-mail _____

Fax _____

Mail today to:

MORRIS CERULLO WORLD EVANGELISM
San Diego: P.O. Box 85277 • San Diego, CA 92186
Canada: P.O. Box 3600 • Concord, Ontario L4K 1B6
U.K.: P.O. Box 277 • Hemel Hempstead, Herts HP2 7DH
Website: www.mcwe.com • **E-mail:** morriscerullo@mcwe.com
For prayer 24 hours a day, 7 days a week, call: **1(858)HELPLINE**

There is a greater anointing upon me now than ever before to pray for your needs.

Never before, in my more than 56 years of frontline ministry have I carried a deeper burden for the Body of Christ than I do now.

I have prayed, fasted, interceded, agonized and fought spiritual warfare against satanic powers...

and God gave me a vision!

God said..."Place the needs of my people upon the altar before My Presence...Jesus is praying for all their needs to be met!"

A vision of Jesus Christ, our Great High Priest, praying for all your needs.

God said, *"Place the needs of my people upon the altar before My Presence. Jesus is praying for all their needs to be met."*

Every need, every disease, every family problem, every circumstance...God wants me to lift your need to Jesus to pray for you. Do not delay. Write all your needs on the following page and mail it to me today!

For Prayer 24 hours a day, 7 days a week, call:
1(858) HELPLINE